the U.S. *economy*

by John Davenport

This book seeks to describe some of the main achievements of the U.S. economy and what we owe to the free market system and to the concept of limited as against unlimited government. Its thesis is that, while government must lay down the framework for economic activity, the main source of our progress comes from the work of individuals and free associations of all kinds. Having defined what we owe to the market, the book discusses the nature of profit and loss, the achievements of the American farmer, and the relation of wages to employment.

It seeks to define the role of monetary and fiscal policy, calls for a reduction in federal government spending as well as in taxes, and outlines the main problems facing us in the external world of trade, aid, and international investment. In a concluding chapter Mr. Davenport emphasizes that the main challenge to American society lies not in economics, but in the view we take of man and his destiny.

Today, when our nation's economic policy touches each of us more than ever before, this book will serve as a useful primer for every concerned citizen.

the U.S.
economy

the U.S. *economy*

JOHN DAVENPORT

HENRY REGNERY COMPANY
Chicago   1964

23607

To Marie

"The economy is the front line
of the defense of liberty. . . ."

WILHELM ROEPKE,
A Humane Society

————————————————

Preface

We live in an eclectic age in which the task of reconciling divergent ideas is legitimately, I think, an important concern of the American citizen. This book is a small attempt to reconcile the way of the free market economy with the legitimate role of government to the end that, in the words of Sir Alec Douglas-Home, "private enterprise will be enterprising [and] the government will govern."

Sir Alec may or may not be governing when this book appears, but his phrase succinctly summarizes the essential premise of our economic and political institutions. How well we preserve those institutions depends in part on continuing what President Kennedy, speaking under the elms of New Haven, defined as the all-important "dialogue."

It is perhaps worth pointing out that this book appears while the U.S. is still enjoying a prolonged and indeed unique prosperity, making it easier to celebrate the American accomplishment in all its amplitude. I should be happily surprised if this state of affairs continued indefinitely. Those old enough to recall the twenties will discount easy talk of a reces-

sion-proof "new era" (even though the *unique* combination of circumstances which produced the great
depression are not likely to recur). More proximately,
our increasing military involvement in the Far East
could spark inflation and bring with it political pressure for ill-advised government controls. Yet I would
also hold that in these matters we have learnt something from experience, and this is one more reason
for trying to take the long view.

When a book goes to the printer it is inevitable, I
suppose, to wish that it could have been done differently. Specifically, I am acutely aware that the discussion of the American monetary problem which
appears sketchily in Chapters VI and VIII is inade-
quate to the issues involved; and I should like to
pay explicit tribute here to those few economists like
Professors Friedman and Aaron Director of the University of Chicago and my associate Michael Heilperin, who have tried at least to stretch our minds on
this subject (albeit in opposite directions). For the
strengthening and reshaping of our monetary institutions remain, in my judgment, the great and unfinished business of the business enterprise economy.

For the rest, I owe thanks to *Fortune* magazine for
its generosity in giving me time and overtime to
write, and for allowing me freely to plagiarize from
articles and editorials which I had previously written
or edited for the magazine. My remarks on taxation,
for instance, draw heavily on essays written by my
associates Max Ways and Gilbert Burck. I also am

indebted to Professor Patrick Boarman of Bucknell University and others for having consented to read the original manuscript and pass on advice. Finally, I owe an enduring debt to Friedrich Hayek, and to the Mont Pelerin Society, whose deliberations over the years have provided an itinerant journalist with a duty-free seminar.

Despite such assistance, tangible and intangible, one inevitably discovers in trying to write about a great subject that one walks, as in *Pilgrim's Progress*, with "a very brisk lad . . . and his name was Ignorance." Yet if one knew at the beginning all that one is conscious of not knowing at the end, publishers would, I suppose, be more hard-pressed than they are today for manuscripts. Fortunately, the subject of the American political economy is not easily exhausted. Today we know some of the issues. Tomorrow we may be blessed with the wisdom to define policies worthy of our tradition and future.

New York May, 1964   JOHN DAVENPORT

Table of contents

the U. S.
economy

CHAPTER I

Of the American achievement

"But westward, look, the land is bright."
—ARTHUR HUGH CLOUGH

"THE PROGRESS OF CIVILIZATION," wrote the philosopher Alfred North Whitehead in his *Science and the Modern World*, "is not wholly a uniform drift towards better things." Whatever its relevance to the development and meaning of modern science, Whitehead's dictum is surely applicable to the times in which we live. In the twentieth century, now two-thirds completed, Western civilization has endured not only the shock of two world wars, not only the arrival of forces and techniques that could be still more destructive, not only the rise of communism and fascism, but it has likewise had to face the dissolution of old faiths and beliefs which once were all but taken for granted. Among these beliefs, none has been subject to sharper discount than the idea of inevitable and beneficent progress. Progress, we can see today, is not something that can be assumed

I

to be in the natural order of things. Much less can it be equated with mere material advance. If civilization is to progress, its advance must perforce be measured by superior values—the values implicit in morality, in aesthetics, and in religion. The realization of these values is by no means self-evident in the secular, democratic, and industrialized society that stretches around us.

From this point of view it would be foolish to take too much comfort from the indubitable success of what, for want of a better term, I shall call the American political economy. It would likewise be foolish to discount this success too severely. If one casts one's mind back to the conditions that existed as late as the mid-nineteenth century in American and European cities as they adjusted to the industrial revolution, one will not be too embarrassed by what today is known as the "urban sprawl." If one has smelt the *barriadas* on the outskirts of many a South American city, one will not be disposed to look down one's nose at the contribution made to more decent living by sanitation and plumbing, by the electric light bulb and the thermostat-controlled furnace, by the multiple means of mass communication, or even by the tail-finned car.

The great disparity that today exists between the so-called advanced and the underdeveloped countries is indeed real. We would scarcely be better off if no country had advanced economically and all were on the same dreary plain. The early Pilgrims were wont to set aside a day of thanksgiving because their handful of seed-corn had sprouted on a rocky shore. Without mistaking material for spiritual progress, one must still occasionally entertain a thought of thanks for the American economy in all its amplitude and complexity—the steel mills of the Monongahela, the oil fields of Louisiana, the wide oceans of grain stretching across west Kansas and Nebraska, the advent of biochemical drugs, sold casually next to the soda fountain, the development of a vast wholesale and retail marketing system whereby the output of farm and factory is made available to the housewife or paterfamilias even though Broadway has lamented the death of a salesman.

More generally, it is no mean achievement that a country, possessing less than 7 per cent of the world's land area and some 6 per cent of its population, produces over a third of the world's goods, and has since World War II poured out billions in food, clothing, and tools for the reconstruction of Europe and the aid of many less fortunate nations. It is again a sign of progress, not decadence, that, thanks to the march of technology and investment, real wages in the U.S. have quadrupled in the past century, that the average family income in the U.S. in the 'sixties exceeds $7,500, and that the number of families in the middle income group has steadily multiplied. In the jargon of the times, the U.S. has ceased to be a pyramidal society "with fetters for the crew and spices for the few" and has become a diamond-shaped society which, despite a still inordinate amount of poverty at the bottom, nevertheless has been alleviating want and distress. More than a hundred years ago Karl Marx predicted, in the Communist Manifesto, that industrialization was bound to create an ever-swelling proletariat which soon or late would topple the whole capitalistic system. In ways not vouchsafed to Marx or, for that matter, Khrushchev to understand, the U.S. has refuted that prediction, creating, if not a classless, at least a class-fluid society in which the benefits of material progress have been ever more widely shared.

2.

The practical business at hand is how to consolidate and maintain this humane advance, which on the record has yielded far more than material progress. To do so involves choice as to economic policy. It also involves understanding of the economic and political system which has brought us this far. The most obvious characteristic of this system is the rise and importance of private business enterprise, which has contributed so signally to the American success story. But we also live in a day of big government, whose defense expenditures alone are now some three times the annual sales of General Motors. Taking both of these factors into account, it is popular to describe the American system as a "mixed economy" in which both business and government are kept in harmonious relationship. Let us make a deep bow to the so-called "private sector" of the economy. But let us also not forget the importance of what has become known as the "public sector."

Yet it turns out on analysis that the term "mixed economy" is a good deal less precise, and hence less useful, than is commonly assumed. Sometimes, as indicated above, the term simply means that in the U.S. today we have a lot of government as well as non-government activity—a truism which may be confirmed by a glance at the national income figures, if the bite of the tax collector has not already brought it to our attention. Again, the term may denote a reputedly happy state of affairs, where Western governments exercise more power over men's lives than they did in the nineteenth and early twentieth centuries but less power than the totalitarian regimes of, say, Soviet Russia or Red China. More frequently than not, the term "mixed economy," while purporting to be a description of things as they are, carries with it strong policy over-tones. Since the U.S. has waxed great at a time when government has obviously expanded its influence, there can be little danger in further accretions of power. Those who oppose such accretion may be conveniently dismissed as reactionaries looking back-ward to a vanished day of *"laissez faire."* Those who accept such accretion are riding, if not the "wave of the future," at least the ground swell of the present.

They are men who have rid their minds of old myths and prejudices and are willing to face current complex realities in a courageous and "sophisticated" way.

Whatever may be said for this approach to contemporary problems in terms of forensic tactics, it is not likely to answer the kind of questions about economics and politics which thoughtful men wish to see illuminated. Old verities, it may be observed, do not necessarily become myths simply because they do not happen to have come off last year's academic production line. More surely, there is something a bit mean and degrading in portraying the American republic and the free economy which sustains it as a kind of convenient halfway station between the extremes of weak and irresolute government, on the one hand, and totalitarian rule, on the other. More surely still, apologists for the "mixed economy" get themselves and their country into trouble by regarding, as they all too often seem to regard, the sphere of government and the sphere of private initiative and free collaborative effort as so many *interchangeable parts,* so that it does not really matter very much if we have a little more of the one and a little less of the other. Involved here is a deep misunderstanding of the *qualitative* differences which separate the acts of government, on the one hand, from the actions of individuals and free associations on the other. Until this misunderstanding is cleared up, advocacy of a mixed economy will almost certainly lead to mixed-up policies.

3.

If we are to avoid such a mix-up, we must, I think, try to view man's political and economic problem in somewhat larger perspective than debate about the functions and specific acts of government entails. As Barry Goldwater has reminded us in *The Conscience of a Conservative,*[1] few important questions in politics or economics can be answered without reference to a prior question: namely, the nature of man, the whole man, and not just this or that aspect of his being. If, as the Marxists suppose, man is simply a material phenomenon, shaped and pulled this way and that by his environment, then we may suppose that some kind of "social engineering" can minister to his needs, and it is only a step from here to giving government unlimited powers. But if man is something different, if he is endowed with the power of choice and volition and a sense of good and evil, then a very different approach to the questions of political economy follows. This is not to say that a full-blown detailed social structure can be deduced from metaphysical premises, for it is notorious that men with the same religious beliefs, for instance, can arrive at very different political conclusions. What is

1 (New York: Macfadden-Bartell Corp., 1960).

tolerably clear is that just as progress implies the realization of values and standards, so too these are basic to the great issues of politics and indeed of economics. In Plato's *Republic,* Socrates opens the discourse with a discussion of justice and the role of the state in achieving it. It is not long before the dialogue is at grips with a more profound question—namely, the nature of the Good, and specifically the good of man.

Among the good things which man has cherished over the ages but to which Plato paid far too little attention is freedom or liberty, defined simply as freedom from external coercion. So defined, freedom appears as a purely negative goal, definitely subsidiary to the pursuit of virtue. The potential conflict in aim is more apparent than real. For if man is to pursue virtue in a practical sense—if the exercise of his free will and choice is to be effective—then it is essential that his sphere of private activity not be invaded and invalidated by the action of others, whether individually or in association. It is this freedom from external coercion that distinguishes the free society from the slave society; and the reduction of coercion, in so far as possible, may be taken as a practical political goal, uniting men of widely different philosophic outlooks. It is the obvious and proclaimed goal of the traditional libertarian (as distinguished from the modern political liberal). It is likewise the goal of the modern conservative, in so far as he seeks to preserve the best of our tradition and heritage. That tradition and heritage no doubt includes much more than devotion to liberty, as defined above. It scarcely can be conceived as including less.

But the enlargement of the scope of freedom and the reduction of coercion turn out to be among the more difficult goals to achieve. The reason lies in the fact that if A is to be protected in his private rights against B, then some superior instrument must be found for enforcing such protection. The instrumentality is in fact the government or the state, which assumes the very kind of coercive authority which we are seeking to reduce. Failure to stress the fact that government by its nature is coercive lies at the root of many of our modern difficulties. Yet indubitably this is the case. Behind most acts of government lies the police authority. This is most clearly seen in the maintenance of internal law and order and the administration of justice. It is also obvious in the case of national defense. Governments over the years have assumed many other functions—the maintenance of national monetary systems, the provision of public works, the extension of educational facilities. Some of these functions may be regarded as public services which, if voted by the people, seem to involve little interference with our liberties. Yet the fact is that behind them the element of coercion is present, if only in that they must be paid for by the taxing power. The power to tax can be the power to destroy. More broadly, the power to tax has behind it

the authority to send men to jail if they do not pay
their tax bills.

It is because government by definition must be
coercive, and must in its sphere have a *monopoly* of
such coercion, that the need arises for limiting its
authority. One answer which civilized men have
found for so doing lies in the concept of law. By the
"rule of law" we may mean that behind all legislative
acts and constitutions there is a higher law, grounded
in the nature of the universe and ultimately in its
Creator. This idea lies behind the theory of "natural
rights." More generally, law implies universality and
avoidance of the arbitrary. As Friedrich Hayek has
shown in his *Constitution of Liberty*,[2] it is the nature
of law to be general and applicable to all citizens
equally. If strong insistence is put on this point, governments will in fact be limited in what they can
legitimately do and cannot do. It is possible, for instance, to draw up universally applicable laws against
murder, theft, and other undesirable acts. It is not
possible to draw up universally applicable laws as to
how an economy shall be run. If we go back to wartime experience, for instance, it is notable that the
first act of the price control authorities was to freeze
all prices—a universal edict. Within weeks, and
indeed days, the authorities had to begin shifting
prices around, letting this one rise and that one
remain stable. In short, what at first appeared to be a

2 (Chicago: University of Chicago Press, 1960).

law became an open gate for purely discretionary and arbitrary authority.

4.

It is the great blessing of Americans that they inherit a government founded by men who were well aware of the need for mitigating such discretion and who made it their business to limit the powers of the government they were creating. Taking a broad view of man's natural rights, the founders of the Republic saw clearly that protection of these rights entailed effective government, and their immediate problem was to unite the several states in a more perfect union. But in perfecting the union they were also acutely aware of the need for dispersing power lest a new tyranny arise. Through the principle of federalism, and of delegated powers, no less than through the principle of checks and balances as between legislature, executive, and judiciary, they created what Lord Bryce was careful to call, not the American nation, but the American Commonwealth. And by capping the Constitution with the Bill of Rights and specifying that powers not delegated to the central government "are reserved to the States respectively, or to the people," they went perhaps as far as man has ever gone in devising the perfect instrument for government by and of free men.

Yet it can scarcely be doubted that the success of

the American experiment in producing a society where liberty flourishes under the rule of law has been dependent on another circumstance—namely, the development of a type of economy which by its nature disperses power and decision. At the root of this economy is the institution of private property, which John Locke and his followers took to be a basic human right no less important than freedom itself. Why Jefferson in the Declaration substituted "Life, Liberty, and the Pursuit of Happiness" for Locke's earlier formulation of "life, liberty, and property" is a matter of some dispute among scholars, but too much importance should not be attached to the change in wording. As Gottfried Dietze has recently pointed out in his book, *In Defense of Property*,[3] the complaint which the Declaration lodges against King George involves the infringement of property rights no less than other human rights. And the modern tendency to try to draw a distinction between property rights, on the one hand, and human rights, on the other, is highly misleading. Freedom of the press, for instance, is impossible without freely owned private presses. Freedom of assembly comes to an end where government owns or can shut down the assembly halls. Freedom of speech, at the least, entails that the speaker has enough private resources on hand to see him through the potentially painful results of disagreement with authority. Freedom to produce and to earn a living is impossible if govern-

[3] (Chicago: Henry Regnery Company, 1963).

ment lays hands on the basic means of production. This truth, missed by Marx in his haste to usher in a new utopia, would scarcely have had to be argued in 1787. It should not have to be argued today. It is no coincidence that the very word "property" is closely related to the words "proper" and "propriety." And without exaggeration it can be said that belief in, and protection of, property is the hallmark of civilization.

But while property and wide dispersion of property rights are no doubt the foundation of the free economy, they are not its only characteristics. The second great institution which has allowed the U.S. to develop in freedom and under limited government is the *market,* defined in simplest terms as freedom to exchange goods and services of all kinds. Such exchange has of course characterized the most primitive of societies, whether effected through barter or through monetary media such as wampum or cattle hides. What is true, however, is that freedom of exchange becomes more and more imperative as society becomes more complex. In a relatively simple agrarian community the need for free exchange and the market is relatively limited. But as production becomes diversified, as human labor is separated in both space and time from the ultimate consumer, then the means of binding the two together becomes more and more important, and the institution of the market becomes the essential highway to free collaboration.

It so happens that the great American experiment in limited government was launched at precisely the time when this truth was becoming manifest. In the seventeenth and well into the eighteenth century, while European governments were committed to private property rights, they were also committed to mercantilism, favoring the limitation of trade and exchange. Indeed, when Colbert, Louis XIV's minister of commerce, came to codify French textile regulations of this period, it took 2,200 quarto pages to do the job. In Britain, the government was committed to trying to regulate the trade of the colonies in a way to favor British domestic manufacturers. Against this whole mercantilist tradition the New World was in revolt. Thus it came about that when the new American republic was formed, its founders took for granted that freedom of exchange, at least within the limits of the new country, was as basic as private property ownership. The protective tariff would come, but the mind-set of the times was against specific government regulation of economic affairs. Political and economic freedom were assumed to be inseparable.

The consequences of this assumption were profound and led on to a period of spectacular economic development. The history of that development is well known. What is important to grasp is why the free market is a superior form of organization in any dynamic society. The first reason concerns efficiency. Adam Smith, whose *Wealth of Nations* appeared in the same year as the Declaration of Independence, had seen that increased production flows from increased division of labor and that such division necessitates exchange. It was a profound insight. As Walter Lippmann summed up the matter in *The Good Society*[4]: "The market is not something invented by businessmen and speculators for their profit, or by the classical economists for their intellectual pleasure. The market is the only possible method by which labor that has been analyzed into separate specialties can be synthesized into useful work. . . . For the division of labor and its regulation in markets are two inseparable aspects of the same process of producing wealth, and the failure to understand that truth is a sure sign of a failure to understand the technical principle of production in the modern world."

But not only the technical principle. The fundamental economic problem of man is, after all, not just to produce more wealth; it is how to produce the goods and services which people want at the right time and at the right place and in the right amounts. The virtue of the market is that it solves this problem in the only way it can be solved if our goal is human liberty and the limitation of government power. In a market economy the consumer, not the producer, is king. It is his bidding which directs production and hence investment into the channels

[4] (Boston: Little, Brown and Company, 1943; New York: Grosset & Dunlap Universal Library, 1956).

where demand is strongest, and even the largest corporation must respond to this demand or go under. It is because this is true that the rise of the great corporation, while surely changing the system, has not altered its fundamental characteristics. The virtue of the market is that it responds to a kind of balloting in the economic arena, which in the long run may be more important than the occasional vote which the citizen casts at the polls.

But there is still a third contribution of the market which receives less attention. It involves the problem of human knowledge. It is the assumption of those who favor an expansion of government control over economic life that men are extraordinarily wise and farsighted. This is not the case. The knowledge of individual men, whether they be ordinary citizens or officials, is highly limited. We cannot foresee today everything that will happen tomorrow. No single mind is capable of understanding all the elements that go into the productive process, especially as this process is constantly being affected by new inventions. The virtue of the market is that it puts small and limited knowledge to work. The consumer knows what he wants in a way that cannot be guessed by some one sitting in high authority. The factory manager knows how to produce this or that product in the cheapest way. It is the assumption of the Rationalists that the human reason can comprehend all the complexities of life. It is because this assumption is false that the market becomes ever more essential the more complex society becomes.

5.

Despite these credentials, the market in modern times has come under increasing attack by those who favor some species of government planning. This term requires definition. It is obvious that in one sense planning is at a premium in the free economy. Individuals plan. Corporations plan. Governments must plan their expenditures and taxes, and what is even more important, must lay down the broad framework or ground rules under which enterprise operates. When one speaks of overhead government planning, however, one means something different. It is the premise of such planning that government should not only manage its own budget but should, so to speak, budget out how the resources of society are to be used. Whereas in the market economy individuals and corporations plan for themselves, it is the essence of government planning that the authorities in question plan for everybody. And whereas in the market economy planning is largely voluntary, the characteristic of government planning is that it is backed by the full power of the state, implying, as we have seen, the use of coercive authority.

The consequences are most clearly illustrated in the case of Soviet Russia, which blundered into central planning in a curious way. Karl Marx was a man in a hurry. While advocating government ownership of the means of production, he apparently gave little thought as to what would happen on the morning after the means of production were seized. This problem devolved upon Lenin and his associates, and there is evidence that they were at first appalled by their task. Indeed, it is said that at one point Lenin asked one of his associates for a five year plan for "twenty or thirty or fifty power stations . . . to give the masses a shining unimpeded prospect to work for."[5] Whether apocryphal or not, the story suggests that much central planning is pure improvisation and lacks any clear criteria as to how resources should be deployed. More seriously, once a plan has been invented, the masses are not apt to follow it unless impelled by *force majeure*. Russia's famous five-year plans can and do roughly direct the economy. They can and have built up Russia's military power and its achievements in space. But they are not responsive to popular choice as to what goods should be produced, and they are enforced from the top down by dictate.

While Marxist socialism has had little direct effect on the U.S., the lure of central planning has had wide influence. One reason, no doubt, has been the effect of two world wars. For war and preparations for war do yield an order of priorities, laid down by

[5] In John Jewkes, *Ordeal by Planning* (New York: The Macmillan Company, 1948).

the military, as to what is to be produced. Moreover, in war people are willing to accept an extraordinary degree of government regulation. It is no coincidence, indeed, that when the U.S. made its most ambitious peacetime experiment in planning under the ill-fated NRA administration of the first Roosevelt regime, it drew on the wisdom and techniques of Baruch's War Industries Board of World War I. Yet the experiment of the NRA amply demonstrates that, without wartime priorities, the attempt to plan production from the center runs into insuperable difficulties. Men in Washington cannot know what should be produced, when, and in what quantities any better than men in Moscow. Inevitably, they turn in a democracy to the leaders of industry and labor to help them execute their design. In effect, the NRA was an attempt to enforce a government-sponsored cartel system. Central planning of this kind does not give people what they want. It is a surrender to entrenched producers and to what Walter Lippmann has called "the polity of pressure groups."

The rise of great pressure groups in the U.S., including powerful unions and various farm organizations, has encouraged the idea that in one way or another they can solve the economic problem. Let big labor, big business, and the farmer get together under the government roof and we can, so the argument runs, create a form of economic organization that is superior to the competitive market. Yet the defects of such organization are clear enough. In the first place, the will of the consumer is shoved aside. Production will go forward according to what producers want rather than what the buying public wants. But in the second place, those who place their faith in this kind of organization of our society are driven into immense political difficulties, where government either abdicates its just powers or overenlarges them or, paradoxically, does both. For great pressure groups generally feed, and are fed by, special government privileges and dispensations. The protective tariff comes to mind in the case of industry, and exemption from antitrust laws is in point in the case of labor. In such cases government, so to speak, delegates out special powers, and it is on these that the groups grow. Thereafter comes the reckoning. For, having ceded out power, government to rule at all must acquire more authority. In his book, *American Capitalism: The Concept of Countervailing Power*,[6] John Kenneth Galbraith takes comfort from the assumption that the groups will somehow "countervail" each other. What he fails to stress is that soon or late big government will have to be invoked as a final countervailing force to these private interests. The social theory of pressure group organization is in fact dangerously reminiscent of the theory of the corporate state as popularized by Mussolini in the 'twenties. The results of such experiments are too fresh in our minds to need much comment.

6 (Boston: Houghton Mifflin Company, 1956).

6.

What this comes down to is that if the great ideal of human liberty under law is to survive and prosper, we must cleave to certain enduring principles, adapting them, no doubt, to the changing complexities of the times in which we live but upholding them nonetheless. Liberty under the law implies strong but limited government. Such government in its turn implies the expansion, not the constriction, of the free market. The two tasks are in fact complementary to each other. A government that seeks to manipulate the minutiae of economic life will soon find itself seeking to dictate that life. At the same time it must be reasserted that the market cannot exist, and never has existed, without a governmental framework. For it depends on the protection of property rights, on the enforcement of private contract, on a functioning money system, on a structure and envelope of law which it is the business of government to supply.

What we need here is perhaps what an older generation of economists referred to as an "agenda" and "non-agenda" for public or governmental policy. As we have implied, the agenda for government is indeed a large one, and if governments in our day fulfilled even their minimal functions, they would not lack duties to keep officials busy. At the level of federal responsibility in the U.S. it is no small thing for the government to care for the common defense, to conduct the nation's foreign policy, to protect the in-

tegrity of the dollar, and to fulfill its judicial function; and at the state and local level the list of services which need to be performed is a long and expansive one. The tragedy and the foolishness of our
day is that elective officials seldom feel constrained
to rest within these boundaries; and so, for example, a
city government whose police force is unable to protect homes from burglary, rape, and dope peddlers
involves itself in a vast hue and cry about the fluori-
dation of water! More generally, we are bound to get,
not just big government, which we may need, but
bad government if we lose the vital distinction between the state as lawgiver and the state as an engine
of constant intervention. As the British economist
John Jewkes has stressed, government should work
"with the tide" of the price-profit system, not
against it. We have sketched in a general way why
this system is essential to freedom and humane collaboration. Let us now take a closer look at how the
process works in detail and take account of the curiously popular notion that, while the market may
have served its purpose in the past, it is no longer
really operative in twentieth-century America.

CHAPTER II

Of the meaning of the market

"The plans and the price system should be pushing in the
same direction and not against each other."
— JOHN JEWKES, *The Myth of Planning*

To HEROES OF SPACE, as to others before them,
the City of New York provides a lavish welcome—
the ticker-tape parade through the canyons of Wall
Street, a stop at City Hall where amenities are ex-
changed with the Mayor, and thereafter a further
motorcade rush uptown to a ceremonial lunch at the
Waldorf-Astoria. Whatever may be said of this ritual
as an acclaim to great deeds accomplished, it leaves
something to be desired as an introduction to this
great world metropolis. For the mystery and miracle
of New York, as is the case with other large cities,
is not to be found in its skyscrapers, its civic center,
or its banquet halls, but rather in a phenomenon so
commonplace and so much taken for granted that it
rarely receives attention. This phenomenon consists
in the fact that some eight million people are able to

23

live together in a space of not much over 300 square miles, which a century and a half ago was mostly rolling farmland. Involved here is a process of human collaboration and coordination of individual effort which in some ways is far more remarkable, though certainly less remarked, than the intricate mechanics and chemistry going into the firing of a rocket, or the safe passage of a space ship around the earth or to the moon.

If we contemplate the city in all of its ramifications, we will no doubt find much that calls for criticism and much that remains to be done. New York has its manifold problems, ranging from snarled traffic to bitter race relations which flare now and again into the open. Yet New York likewise represents an extraordinary human achievement and points an economic lesson of some significance. Every weekday morning, upwards of four million people turn up at their respective jobs, whether in office or in factory or at a construction project, without much over-all direction from the top. The secretary and the executive, the corner storekeeper and his employees, the construction worker and his foreman are somehow at the right place at the right time in a process that could not possibly be comprehended by any single mind or computer. A recent series of advertisements for New York featured Mayor Wagner sitting in his flag-decked office in City Hall. But the number of persons whom Mayor Wagner knows even on the police force or on the civil service list is, to say the least, limited, and if he

attempted to direct New York's work force, the result would be, not direction, but stagnation. Yet indubitably there must be some directing hand or co-
ordinating agency which meshes the work of one man
with that of another. It is found in the fact that, in
seeking to earn a living, whether through daily wage
or salary, the inhabitants of the city do in fact join in
what may be called spontaneous collaboration. The
earnings of many—all too many—may be inade-
quate; strikes may on occasion hold up the process at
one point or another; but, in general, the wonder is
not in the imperfections of the process but in its
efficiency. What appears to be unplanned and
chaotic gives rise in fact to a kind of dynamic design
or pattern.

The same is true of many other aspects of the city.
Some hours before a majority of New Yorkers are
settling down to their jobs, a remarkable scene begins
to unfold on Piers 27–29 North River, where auction
markets help distribute vegetables and fresh fruits
coming from as far as Africa and Chile, as well as from
California and Florida. Visit one of these markets and
the first impression is one of mere confusion and hub-
bub. Transported by barge from the Jersey shore,
boxes of oranges, apples, pineapples, and grapes are
stacked high along the pier, for quality inspection;
thereafter, bidding begins in four rooms on the second floor, with cries from the buyers mingling with
the auctioneer's steady monotone. In the course of the
bidding, a crate of fancy-grade oranges which opened

at $4.90 may drop to $4.75 before the lot is sold. By each afternoon, however, most of the crates are on their way to chain stores or to wholesalers, who in their turn will sell the produce to the corner grocery store. By this and other similar activities, New York is supplied with some $350,000 of fresh fruit per day in the summertime, and with some $150,000 of fresh vegetables. This is "huckstering" in the classical meaning of the word. It involves large risks for buyers as well as sellers. But it is precisely because these risks are taken that demand and supply are equated through the price mechanism, in a way that would be quite impossible were the city fathers to decide that they could plan and manage the process.

New York is known as "headquarters town" since many of the largest corporations in the U.S. have their central offices here and use the city as a kind of command center. Indeed, it is estimated that in the course of a single day over twenty-four million business calls are placed through New York switchboards. If one steps inside a number of these corporate offices, however, one is impressed by the immense diversity of the command process. There is no central planning bureau that seeks to coordinate what each corporation is doing. The executive committee of Standard Oil Co. of N.J., meeting high up in Rockefeller Center, may be discussing the advisability of opening a new refinery in France or of financing new oil explorations in Saudi Arabia. The executives of U.S. Steel may be worrying about a problem in Gary, Indiana, or in ore-rich Venezuela. The officers of Continental Can may be debating the advisability of increasing or decreasing production in Tonawanda, or of putting up a new plant in Nova Scotia. It is these ramified decisions, sometimes taken after long debate, sometimes taken almost casually and involving only a word-of-mouth order, that determine the kind of investment which U.S. business makes in a single year in new plant and equipment—sometimes running to $40 billion or more. On such investment depend, in the last analysis, the country's productivity and its living standards. Yet again, as in the case of food distribution, no single agency could comprehend, much less direct the end result. It is done through dispersed decisions which only afterward seem to add up to an intelligible pattern.

Finally there is Wall Street with its stock exchanges, over-the-counter market, and investment houses which make New York the financial center of the U.S.—perhaps of the world. Visit the New York Stock Exchange on a weekday morning, and you see only some shirtsleeved men at their trading posts, with other traders milling about in what appears to be considerable confusion. The confusion is deceptive. Behind the traders on the floor is an intricate system of brokerage offices through which buy and sell orders for equities from persons perhaps thousands of miles away are executed with no more than a phone call for security. In the course of a single "normal" day, some 2.5 million shares change hands on the New York Stock Exchange alone, reflecting the precise evaluation of owners and would-be owners. Do not believe that these judgments of the owners are irrelevant to the corporate executives of the companies whose shares are traded. On the contrary, how Wall Street prices an equity is of immense concern to the manager of the corporation in question; and freedom to buy and to sell equities in fact closely links ownership and management together. So, too, when bond traders buy or sell U.S. government securities, the effects are immediately felt in the U.S. Treasury in Washington, if not in the White House.

It is sometimes said that little goes on in Wall Street except the trading of bits of paper. But they are very important bits. For the money market in all its ramifications completes the process by which the savings of a nation are translated into profitable investment, and a change in security values may affect the living and the fortunes of men and women in Pittsburgh or Dubuque, or in Peru and Chile. In Wall Street, perhaps more than anywhere else in the world, one becomes conscious of the profound meaning of a book written a good many years ago by Harry Scherman, *The Promises Men Live By*.[1] For the commitment of money in fact involves promises or bets on a future which no man can foretell with certainty. It likewise involves a mutual trust between contracting parties which seldom comes in for public

1 (New York: Random House, Inc., 1938).

notice. We read of the "scandals" or the swindles of this or that operator. We become impervious to the far more remarkable fact that beneath all the intricacies of monetary transactions there is a foundation of honest dealing without which the whole structure would crumble.

2.

These vistas of New York are sharp and specific reminders of how much we owe to the market process, defined simply as the mutually profitable exchange of services and goods of all kinds. If one lifts one's eyes from New York to the country at large, this process becomes awesomely larger though similar in kind. The New York construction or office worker finding his or her daily place in the scheme of things is the prototype of some 70 million wage and salary employees now gainfully employed throughout the country. The huckstering through which New York is daily supplied with fresh fruit and vegetables is a window on a vastly larger distribution process by which products from farm and factory finally reach the consumer. The New York corporate boardrooms are a small if elegant slice of the activities of millions of business firms, large and small, scattered across the country. The abstruse activity of Wall Street is repeated in Chicago, Philadelphia, Los Angeles, and other cities. Put all this together and the number of transactions taking place daily within the U.S. economy obviously runs into the trillions—uncountable, indeed, as the sands of the sea. Just as no single mind could possibly plan out what takes place in New York, so is it even more naïve to believe that a single human intelligence could devise a plan for the nation. Yet, remarkably, this unplanned and seemingly confused process yields a purposeful order in which the right goods generally turn up at the right place in the right quantities.

This is the wonder of the market, or, more specifically, of the system where production is guided by the free play of prices, profits, and wages in the interests of those who buy the final products and services. What we owe to this system is only imperfectly mirrored in the soaring figures for total output and income, which are the stock-in-trade of current economic analysis—though these figures themselves tell quite a story. In late 1947, at the end of World War II, for instance, gross national product was running at about $245 billion. By the end of 1963 it reached the $600 billion mark and, even if we allow for inflation, it had increased in real terms by some 75 per cent. If we break this $600 billion figure down into its rough components, we find that about $380 billion went to the production of consumer goods ranging from food and clothing to automobiles, washing machines, and other so-called "consumer durables." We find another $87 billion going to gross private domestic investment, which includes not only purchase of

new plant and machinery but upkeep of existing facilities and changes in inventories; and we find another $128 billion representing purchase of goods
and services by governments, federal, state, and local.

Such aggregate statistics, while allowing for a considerable range of error, do on the whole faithfully
record the value of the economy's output, but even so
they scarcely reveal the complexity of decision-making which yields the final result. The consumption
figure indicates the scale of individual purchases. But
it masks the intricate arrangements and price calculations that go into the assembly of a Ford or a Chevrolet, with parts coming from hundreds of independent suppliers; the extraordinary distribution process
which gets the car from factory to showroom, and so
into the hands of the buyer; and the bidding and huckstering that goes on in the multi-million used-car
market. The huge investment figure totals the flow
of money spent for maintaining and increasing the
size of our productive plant and apparatus but gives
little inkling of the calculations and risks taken by
thousands of businessmen who are laying out millions
of dollars today against the vagaries and often the disappointments of an uncertain future.

Even the figure for government purchase of goods
and services is somewhat deceptive. On the one hand,
it omits many types of government payments (social
security, interest on the federal debt, etc.) which go to
swell government spending at federal, state, and
local levels, and thus minimizes the role of govern-

ment in our lives. On the other hand, the national product figures for government operations tell us little of government's own dependence on suppliers who are purchasing their component parts and materials in distant markets. In the matter of defense, to take only one example, the military may initiate the process by which a prime contractor like General Electric agrees to manage the construction of a rocket. But into this costly product goes the work of hundreds of smaller firms which are guided by the cost-price and profit calculus. Without that calculus the computers of the Pentagon would have little to bite on, and the economy as a whole, taken in all its complexity, would lack its essential coordination.

3.

Add in the fact that the U.S. is by no means self-sufficient, but vitally dependent on imports, exports, and foreign capital movements, and it is probably fair to say that the *scope* of the American market system, in its international and domestic ramifications is larger and more far-flung today than at any time in history. Yet curiously this is not the popular view, or at least the view of an influential number of critics and commentators. In their view, the U.S. did indeed wax great in the nineteenth century through the expansion of the market, but this expansion is now drawing to a close as the result of irreversible structural changes. Thus in one of his recent books, *The*

American Economic Republic,[2] Mr. Adolf A. Berle states flatly that the U.S. economy, far from being guided by market forces, "is now the result of state-directed planning." Elsewhere he has argued that "perhaps half" the prices in the U.S. are indirectly set by government. From this it follows that those who celebrate the market system are really deluding themselves, and that we would all be better off if we recognized the great changes that have taken place, especially since the 'thirties, and "institutionalized" even further government intervention. For instance, Berle suggests that since large wage and price decisions affect the public interest, it would be a good thing if the President's Council of Economic Advisers were empowered to advise officially on major wage and price changes. For the Council, he thinks, is in a position to have objective knowledge on these subjects.

It is not hard to see in this kind of suggestion a hankering for the kind of overhead planning of production whose general defects we noted in the previous chapter. Nor is it hard to show that if the government were really given this kind of power it would be driven to using a type of wartime control to make its "advice" stick. What is striking about this kind of suggestion is the new twist which Berle and others give for adopting this method of economic organization. The proponents of socialism, fascism, and central planning have in the past based their

2 (New York: Harcourt, Brace & World, Inc., 1963).

case for control on the idea that the market is a chaotic way of doing business and that therefore we *ought* to find a different method. Berle's argument is that, whatever may be said for the market's accomplishments in the past, it has already been obsoleted by the forces of history; hence all efforts to free up the economy or to reduce needless government intervention in it are really irrelevant. This, if true, is an immensely important finding and constitutes a far more damaging challenge to rational public policy than any of those so far considered.

Yet on analysis it turns out that this seemingly hard-headed approach to the economy includes some very woolly reasoning. Sometimes, in making their case that the free market is today moribund and passé, the critics simply point to the fact that government spending, as indicated above, is indeed huge by any past standard and so, by implication at least, we might as well make it bigger. This involves the old logical fallacy of confusing what is with what ought to be; but, even if we pass over this fallacy, the government spending figures alone do not quite make the case being argued. As noted, government procurement itself is vitally dependent on market forces and on what we have called the market calculus, and were this absent, even the defenses of the country would be in sorry shape. In addition, the fact that total government spending at all levels and of all kinds now runs to about a third of total national product does not mean that government is running the whole economy. We are indeed in danger of what the German economist Wilhelm Roepke has called "fiscal socialism," but we have not yet passed the point of no return.

More importantly, the Berle thesis fails to draw a proper distinction between what governments have always done and must do if an enterprise economy is to flourish, and what they should not do. The City of New York has not gone socialist because for a good many years now we have expected the city fathers to pave and clean the streets, and to provide for sewage disposal as well as a fresh water supply; none of these things explains the wonder of New York's co-ordination, already touched upon. At the federal level, the founders of the Republic themselves put in place some mighty important government timbering when they inserted into the Constitution the inter-state commerce clause, without which there would be no continental market, the clauses setting up the federal judicial system, and the currency clause, which still underlies our monetary system. It is true that through the Federal Reserve System as well as the budget, the federal government exercises wide powers that affect, and consciously affect, employment and total output. But it is not true, as Berle asserts, that whether he knows it or not the owner of an equity or a bond "is now at the mercy of the political state," unless we wish to infer that the political state fully controls our lives because it has a large responsibility for the issue of money in which *all* price, profit, and wage transactions are made. At this point we should have surely driven the argument about government power to its *reductio ad absurdum*.

Failure to distinguish between necessary governmental framework and unnecessary interventionism is most clearly illustrated in the matter of pricing. As we shall presently see, the government has made much trouble for itself and everybody else by trying to prop up certain farm prices above their market level—causing unmanageable surpluses and constant pressure for more controls. But there is nothing detrimental to the market in the fact that, where monopolies are the most efficient means of output, as in the case of the utilities, the setting of rates should be subject to regulation. More broadly, the U.S. has gained on net balance through the antitrust laws, and might well gain more were these applied to organized labor as well as to industry. But such encouragement of competition is something quite different from the suggestion that the government should help set, whether through its Council of Economic Advisers or other agencies, the terms of important wage contracts and the prices of the industries affected. The latter is a way to jam and fatally damage the market process. The former can broaden, or should broaden, the highway over which goods and services of all kinds reach the consumer at least cost, and so enlarge *his* options over what he chooses to buy or not buy.

4.

But it is just here that we discover that critics of
the market have, so to speak, a second string to their
bow. Even with the antitrust laws in operation, it is
asserted that the economy has lost its competitive
character due to the rise of big business. Today, on
some figures, the 200 largest manufacturing companies in the U.S. account for some 40 per cent of
sales. It is certainly true that over the years great ag-
gregates of wealth have come into being, and in the
process General Motors is surely a different kind of
enterprise from those common in the days of Adam
Smith. There are undoubtedly dangers in this kind
of concentration, and few would belittle them. At
the same time, it is easy to distort the evidence. Big
businesses are vitally dependent on smaller businesses for their supplies, and the Department of
Commerce estimates that there are in the U.S. some
4,755,000 business firms, great and small, incor-
porated and non-incorporated. In 1962, to take a
recent year, some 387,000 businesses were discon-
tinued, but some 430,000 came into being to have
their try at the risks and rewards of serving the consumer. This does not on the face of it look like the
demise of the competitive business system.

The claim that competition is dying out is generally supported by making the academic distinction
between what is called "pure" and what is called

"imperfect" competition. Pure competition is a condition in which there are so many sellers of a product that no one of them can affect its price, and where each one of them takes the going price for granted. This is the condition which still rules in many agricultural markets, and which used to rule in all of them before government price supports were invented. By contrast, "imperfect" competition is a state of affairs where there are few enough sellers so that each one can affect prices by holding down or expanding output. This is the condition which rules in the automobile industry, where there are three big sellers. General Motors does not take the price of its cars as given. Its executives constantly ponder whether the price of a Chevrolet this year should be a little more or less than last year's model. Thus General Motors is in a different position from a farmer selling apples or broccoli.

But how much does this distinction really prove? Actually, it proves very little. Businessmen from time immemorial have believed that they could affect prices somewhat. This was true long before the rise of the modern giant corporation and held in the eighteenth as well as in the nineteenth century—the very period in which Berle and others say that the free market was at its height. Thus if imperfect competition in itself means the decline of the market, it can be argued that there never was a market in the production of many types of goods. This surely proves for too much for the comfort of the critics.

Beyond this, it must be said that if we take competition in a meaningful and not an academic sense, it is still palpable and real throughout the American economy, no matter what the concentration of particular industries. It is indulging in mere semantics to say that the automobile industry is non-competitive. In steel, too, there is intense competition between the eight major firms and the literary hundreds of small suppliers. The same is true of aluminum, which was once dominated by a single company but where there are now at least four great producers. In addition, competition between industries is intense. Aluminum presses against steel and copper, and vice versa. Steel is further pressed when builders erect large buildings with reinforced concrete rather than steel girders. In drugs much is made of the dominance of a few large firms, but nevertheless prices have a way of coming down. Penicillin, which once sold at $250 per gram now sells for 2.5 to 3 cents a gram. One antibiotic rapidly replaces another. Du Pont made a fortune with nylon. But it spends millions each year to develop new products, and should it cease to do so it would soon be out of business.

Thus it turns out that the argument that big business has destroyed the market process is even more suspect than the argument that big government spending *of and by itself* has completely destroyed the system. We must be very careful, of course, not to read too much into this conclusion. It does not tell us that everything is right with the economy. It does free us from accepting both the defeatism of many critics and the prescriptions which they draw from that defeatism. The point is that there is no reason to succumb to this defeatism. We are not in the grip of inevitable historic forces which Marxist materialism has sought to popularize and to propagandize. Ensconced in the Kremlin, Khrushchev may talk of burying capitalism. But it turns out that amidst all the talk he and his planning bureau somehow forgot that the growing of wheat requires fertilizer—something that the U.S. chemical industry supplies without being ordered to do so. The magic catalyst here, as in other areas, is the profit motive. In the next chapter we shall take a closer look at how this catalyst performs, and at how the farmer and the American worker are bound into the collaborative effort of production. It will then be time to turn attention to some of the functions, including the provision of a monetary system, which government must perform if enterprise is to flourish, and to an analysis of the line which separates the welfare state from a government which seeks to promote the general welfare.

CHAPTER III

Of profit and loss

"Profit is merely the index, the proof that production was for use."

—Gustav Stolper, *This Age of Fable*

"THE BUSINESS OF AMERICA IS BUSINESS," remarked Calvin Coolidge, and ever since sophisticates have been ridiculing the Sage of Northampton, Mass., for his cheap and materialistic view of his country. They are, in their way, right. For the business of the United States, from its founding through the first half of the twentieth century, has obviously been more than commercial profit and loss. The "national purpose," however defined—and it is a term that needs careful definition—cannot be confined within the narrow limits of the counting house or the factory. Yet in justification to Coolidge it may also be said that without business and the businessman there never would have been the America which we know today, and the implementation of the national purpose would remain academic small talk. As John Chamberlain has shown in *The Enterprising*

Americans,[1] a history of American enterprise from colonial times forward, it is the businessman and the risk-taker who in large measure built up this country's agriculture, developed its early manufacturing facilities, laid down the rails between two oceans, ushered in the age of mass production, developed the wonders of electricity and communication, and now stand behind its defenses and probe into outer space. Without its Pepperrells, Cabots, Whitneys, Fords, Rockefellers, Trippes, and Sarnoffs, the American continent might have lain potentially rich yet fallow. These and many other men were the economic decision-makers. To borrow a phrase from Edison, they "pushed the system."

So pervasive, indeed, has been and is the influence of business enterprise that it is and has always been difficult to define its outer limits. "We are literally all workers," remarked Amos Lawrence expansively in the 1850's, "and the attempt to get up a workingman's party is a libel upon the whole population." Just so, it might be said that everybody who takes part in the creative process of production is a businessman; and attempts to define business as the province of corporate tycoons is an affront to common sense and common observation. As we have seen, it is the essence of the market economy to bind together and to coordinate all types of human effort; and if one observes any particular job in progress—say, the tearing down of an old, and the erection of a new, building

[1] (New York: Harper & Row, Publishers, 1963).

—it is difficult to say where the creative function of the workman, the foreman, the manager, and the entrepreneur or businessman begins and leaves off. They are all for the moment engaged on a particular bit of "business" which will, it is to be hoped, eventually serve the community, and the transaction of this business, at the time at least, seems one and indivisible.

Nevertheless, for purposes of analysis it is possible to draw a dividing line which separates out the economic role of the workman and the paid supervisor from that of the businessman or entrepreneur proper. It is found if one asks the simple question: who will suffer the *loss* if the contracting firm in question fails to finish the job on time or in some other way botches the job, and who, alternatively, will make the *profit* if all goes according to schedule and plan? Not the workman, for he will be paid his wages as long as the job continues. Not the salaried supervisor, for he likewise will get his reward. The answer, of course, is that it is the owners of the contracting firm who will reap the rewards or suffer the disappointments of success or failure. It is they who have laid out the money to bring the mason, the carpenter, and the electrician to the spot; it is they who have contracted for a steady flow of materials—concrete, steel, lumber, brick; and, it is they, more importantly, who rent or buy the tools necessary for the undertaking—the pneumatic drills, the bulldozers, the soaring, swaying cranes. All these things represent costs—some variable, some fixed—which, it is hoped, will total something less than the final price for erecting the building. If this hope or gamble proves correct, there will be a residual profit. If it proves incorrect there will be loss, and the firm, if it can withstand the strain, will have to turn to another contract to make good the deficiency.

While this no doubt is an oversimplification of how the construction industry operates, it nevertheless allows us to define the nature of business enterprise with a fair amount of precision. While business in broadest definition is the creative process of making things, business in narrower definition is the act of *organizing* the means of production in a way that will ultimately satisfy buyers or consumers. The reward for undertaking the risks of such organization is profit, defined as the evanescent and residual margin of return between cost and selling price. The word "evanescent" is used advisedly, for in a purely static economy profits as defined above would not long exist. If consumer tastes remained constant, on the one hand, and if no technological developments or inventions occurred, on the other, then there would soon be no room for profits (though there would always be need to pay for supervisory skills). But in the real world such static conditions are never long present. The buying tastes of the public do change from moment to moment and from year to year. New inventions come forward which obsolete old ways of doing things. It is the business of business and the businessman to cope with these changing conditions, and to put them to use in the expectation of profit return.

Put in another way, profit or loss is the result of *uncertainty* about the future which changing tastes and new technologies inevitably create. If everybody were sure today about what would happen tomorrow, there would be no special place for the entrepreneur, and nothing left over for the profit residual. If, to take an extreme example, one were sure this year that there would be demand next year for exactly 100,000 Buick cars priced at $3,400, and if no changes occurred in the costs of making cars, then all risks of manufacturing Buicks would disappear, and costs, including payments for wages, management, and capital, would equal selling price. But such certainty is never present, either on the selling side or the manufacturing side, and the producer in fact always takes a chance which, if correct, is duly rewarded. As the economist Ludwig von Mises has put it: "What makes profit emerge is the fact that the entrepreneur who judges the future prices of the products more correctly than other people do, buys some or all of the factors of production at prices which, even from the point of view of the future state of the market, are too low. Thus the total costs of production—including interest on the capital invested—lag behind the prices which the entrepreneur receives for the product. This difference is entrepreneurial profit."[2]

Profits are thus something quite different from

2 Paper delivered before Mt. Pelerin Society, September, 1951; see also von Mises' *Human Action* (New Haven: Yale University Press, 1949).

other shares of the national income and, on analysis, are not really a share at all, and certainly not a fixed share. They are rather something left over after all other factors have been accounted for. The biggest share of national income logically goes for wages and salaries, which are straight payments for work done or contracted for. Another share of the national income goes for interest, which is the reward, not for risk-taking, but for the willingness of some people to wait and to forego consumption today for a larger reward tomorrow. These lend out their money at short term or at long term, as the case may be, to entrepreneurs who will put it to work. Interest is thus wholly vital to capital formation, but it is a payment that, short of default by the borrower, does not vary from the 4 per cent or 6 per cent promised on the bond. Even dividends, in so far as they represent a normal return on capital tied up in a business, are regarded by economists as something different from "pure" profits, which are, to repeat, something left over after all capital, as well as wage and managerial costs, are paid.

Profits in economic theory are thus something smaller and less calculable than what is shown under this head in the familiar national income statistics, but these latter are nevertheless revealing. For they indicate, as one would expect, that profitability is subject to enormous fluctuations up and down. In 1963, for instance, corporate profits in the U.S. after taxes were reported at $24.6 billion. But in 1932, at the pit of the great depression, profits were actually negative to the tune of $3.4 billion. Some businesses, of course, continued to make money. But in the system as a whole, losses far outran profit. As long as there is any production at all, some wages and salaries will be paid. Profits, however, enjoy no such immunity, and the reward of risk-taking may turn into loss when the market fails to fulfill the expectations of the risk-takers. Fundamentally, the U.S. is not a profit economy. It is a *profit-and-loss* economy, and those who do not emphasize this fact have grossly misrepresented the nature of the so-called "capitalist" system.

Such misunderstanding has been widespread, and attack on profits has come from many quarters. The boldest attack was launched by Karl Marx, who argued that profits were a so-called "surplus value," extorted from the hide of the workingman by greedy capitalists for no useful service performed. But this overlooks the fact that the worker cannot create any "surplus value" over what he receives. The value of his work is his wage, which is fixed by the supply and demand for his services. In many cases, this wage would be non-existent or far lower than it is today were it not that the proper materials and tools have been brought together through which his work can be performed. It is in risking his money for the assembly of these tools, which by definition are scarce, that the entrepreneur performs his most important function from the point of view of the worker and from the point of view of society itself. For the tools have to be made and paid for before wages, or in any case high wages, will be forthcoming. In an advanced economy, production is always "roundabout," involving a large number of steps, such as the erection of a plant or factory, before final goods can come off the line. The more roundabout the process of production becomes, the more need there is for someone to bear the risks of organizing it. The alternative to a profit-and-loss economy is not, as Marx supposed, a worker's paradise. The alternative is either the attempt by government to organize production through total centrist planning, whose defects we examined in a previous chapter, or, in the telling phrase of economist Frank Knight, just plain "chaos."

More current fallacies about profits, and so about business enterprise, are the notions that profits can, on the one hand, be "excessive" and, on the other, that they can be fixed at some "reasonable" level. The first idea runs like a red thread through many political investigations, but has little to commend it. If a business has, for instance, brought forward a new invention which greatly reduces costs, it will for the time being earn profits far in "excess" of its competitors, but such excess is simply a signal that still more capital is needed in this line of production. Under conditions of competition within the industry, or indeed, of inter-industry competition, this new capital will tend to be forthcoming, and the "excessive" profits of the firm originating the invention will under competitive conditions soon be whittled down. The collateral notion, sometimes put forward by businessmen themselves, that while profits should not be excessive, still they should be "reasonable" is equally specious, and can perhaps be even more harmful. For if businesses are to be guaranteed a "reasonable" profit, it will surely not be long before the state or the trade unions assume the task of trying to figure out what this reasonable reward should be. This is an open invitation to reduce all business to the status of the public utilities, with commissions set up to regulate them. The fact is that no business has a "right" to any given level of profits, any more than it has the "right" to any given level of prices. It should charge "what the market will bear," confident that, if it has correctly judged the market and its own costs, some profit may be forthcoming to itself while others may no doubt be taking losses.

It will be argued that in all of the above we have made some large assumptions, which cannot be taken for granted. The first assumption is that competition *does* exist within the American economy on a sufficient scale to discipline all entrepreneurs to the needs of the market place and to the ultimate wishes of the buying public. Enough has been said on this point in the discussion in Chapter II of so-called "pure" and "imperfect" competition where it was argued that in fact competition is intense, even in industries dominated by two or three very large corporations. But there is a second problem raised by the coming of the corporate giant which does call for some further comment. It concerns the relationship of managers and owners.

In all that we have said about profits, we have used the terms "entrepreneur," "capitalist," "businessmen," and "owners of businesses" more or less interchangeably. In earlier days, when all businesses were relatively small and when owners were actually running their concerns, this shorthand would have been justified. But today we live in the midst of, or perhaps in the aftermath of, the so-called "managerial revolution," when the owners of a business, namely, the equity holders, may be far removed from those who make the day-to-day decisions about how much will be invested in new plant, how much will be put away to surplus, what prices will be set, and what wages will be offered. It will be granted that the active managers who make these hard decisions perform a crucial organizing function in our society and so deserve handsome salary reward, which they in fact usually get. But it is more difficult to see how the inheritor of, say, 100 shares of the Standard Oil Company of New Jersey—shares which remain tucked away in his strong box and which may never be used for voting purposes—performs any risk-taking function, or why he receives more than a nominal return corresponding to the relevant rate of interest for lending out his money.

For even if such an owner did wish to share in managerial decisions, the actual setup of large corporations would prevent it. New capital appropriations or a new price policy are not voted at annual stock-holders' meetings, and even if they were the end re-sult would probably be far from salutary. Pure cor-porate "democracy" would likely lead to anarchy, as have experiments in "pure democracy" in the politi-cal sphere. And such reflections have led a number of commentators, no less than adverse critics, to believe that, quite aside from the problem of competition, the rise of the great corporation has completely changed the rules of the profit game. This was one of the themes of *The Modern Corporation and Private Property*,[3] written by Adolf Berle and Gardiner Means in the 'thirties, and it is a theme restressed in Mr. Berle's more recent book, already referred to, *The American Economic Republic*. Divorce of ac-tive management from ownership, Mr. Berle argues, has obsoleted traditional ideas of the entrepreneurial function and, indeed, of the whole concept of the "market economy." And it is because of this belief that the market economy is obsolete that Mr. Berle and others of his persuasion almost take for granted, and, indeed, seem to favor, a perpetual enlargement of government power over the economy.

Now it must be said immediately that even if the so-called divorce of management from ownership were as absolute as the critics make out, there would not *for that reason alone* be a case for increased gov-ernment intervention in the economic process. This

3 (New York: The Macmillan Company, 1935).

would have to be argued on its merits, and, as we have seen, the merits of central government planning are hard to come by. But more pertinently, it must be emphasized that the equity holders of any business do take risks, even though they delegate to management the day-to-day running of the enterprise. For, in effect, they are betting on management's ability to bring the business through good times and bad, and to expand with the years. They are betting on future and indeterminate prospects, and these bets may, of course, be disastrously ill advised, as many an equity owner has had cause to regret.

There was a time when the American Woolen Corporation was blue chip, and considered a necessary prerequisite of any balanced Bostonian portfolio, just as there was a time when a Main Line Philadelphian who did not own shares of the Pennsylvania Railroad was a species of queer duck. Investors in American Woolen, at least, who did not exercise their right and privilege to sell this equity at any time they chose suffered the consequences. Their rock-ribbed estates dwindled in value, while those who did see the writing on the wall and got out into other investments in time benefited. Thus, indirectly at least, all holders of equities do participate in loss no less than in profit, and if they are to be granted the one they remain entitled to the other. The supply of equity capital cannot in practice be neatly compartmentalized according to the contribution made by its suppliers. And when one considers the need for such capital in bringing forward new, and often small, ventures which can challenge the position of the established goliaths, one will not begrudge profit accruing to those who normally take no part in the day-to-day management decisions. They too are making their speculative commitments on an uncertain future, and those commitments are not covered by a Metropolitan life insurance policy.

Indeed, while some critics are indicting the absentee owner as a do-nothing fellow, it is interesting that others imply that he needs more "protection" from the wiles of powerful management. Once again the case breaks down when one considers that no one is forced to hold on to equity shares if he prefers a safer type of security. In fact, the stock markets of the country serve to bind owners and management together in a way all too often overlooked. The owner of 100 shares of Standard Oil of New Jersey may not cut much of a swathe at the annual shareholders' meeting, if he attends it at all. But if he dislikes the way things are going, he possesses a powerful blackball, which can be registered by picking up the telephone and selling his shares. Concomitantly, buyers of equities are every day registering their approval of this or that management as they bid for the stock in question. It is naïve to suppose that the managers themselves pay no heed to this form of balloting. On the contrary, they watch the daily returns almost as avidly as they try to keep track of the varying prices of materials, labor, or capital goods which it is their job to assemble together and use in the most efficient possible way. Journalists who report on the industrial scene rapidly discover that corporate executives take pride in something more than the clattering factories or the silent but active refineries that are under their care. They show you the production lines, and explain the wonders of "automation." But they are ready, too, for the vital question as to whether the automation is in fact paying off. The payoff is in the profits, actual and potential, of the business in question; and these in turn are reflected in the price of the company's stock. While this price may be registered in faraway Wall Street, the executive who does not heed it is the exception to the rule; and he will not, if things go wrong, remain even the exception for very long. Management and ownership (quite aside from the fact that managers are themselves often shareholders) are thus irretrievably bound together. The celebrated "bill of divorcement" between them turns out to be just a bill, not an indictment or a fact.

Thus the present corporate setup in the United States is a manifestation of *delegated* authority on the part of owners, rather than abdication of the responsibilities of ownership. In its own way, business has curiously worked out a representative system of control which resembles what some of us still believe should be the norm for political government —a mean between a spurious and unrealizable "pure" democracy, on the one hand, and some form of autocracy, on the other. The virtue of the system from the point of view of the owners is that they get the benefit of skilled managerial talent, on which they can rely for profitable results. The virtue of the system from the point of view of managers is that, so long as they produce results, they have the backing of an independent body of citizens to whom they are ultimately responsible. Without that backing and responsibility, managers would simply be adventurers on the economic scene, without criteria or purpose for their actions. It is private ownership, however diffused, which gives the business firm its central identity in the changing flux of economic events.

This does not mean that all is well with the modern business system, or ever will be. Big corporations, no less than small ones, make mistakes: a General Dynamics goes temporarily out of control and owners foot the loss. Yet, when all the criticisms and warnings are in, one may well ask whether there is a better way of organizing the means of production than the one to which we are committed. Certainly the alternatives are not enticing, whether we look to the right or left. In Europe, many who once preached the virtues of the cartel system are today hoping that the Common Market will again bring a more beneficent reign of competition between independent establishments. But the evidence from the left is still more revealing. The big news coming out of Soviet Russia is not in the production statistics, which are in fact falling off. The big news is that after nearly half a century of central planning the planners are trying desperately to achieve some way of diversifying and decentralizing the process of economic decision-making. Yet decentralization comes hard in a society where the means of production are not privately owned, particularly when it comes to the crucial question of new capital outlay. It is all very well to pretend that the manager of a factory in Minsk is really independent of Moscow when it comes to the expansion or contraction of his operations. But in the last analysis he will have to adhere to the latest Five Year Plan or the plan itself will miscarry. Where the state owns the means of production the state must dominate, however much it may try to delegate. There is no way of cutting the roots of capitalism and still garnering its fruits.

Those fruits have been considerable, whether we look back to the days of the industrial pioneers or whether we open our eyes to what is going on all around us across the broad land. At the opening of this chapter we offered a short salute to the great "movers and shakers" of the American business scene, but it is not on these that attention really needs to be focused. It is rather the total business process, of which they are the occasional offspring, which presents the marvel; and this process did not end with the laying of rails, the discovery of oil, the rise of Pittsburgh and Detroit, or the burgeoning of the electronics industry with the perfecting of the tiny transistor. Rather enterprise is a continuous and living development, where one competitive breakthrough leads on to another. The justification of the market system lies partly in rising output and proliferation of product. Its larger contribution to American life has been the combining and harmonizing of two things which are most difficult to hold in balance: organization, and the widespread dispersal of power and economic decision-making. Profit is only one factor in the elaborate signaling system we call the free market. But it is a crucial factor. If we live today in an "economic republic" it is not because government has come to, or may wish to, exert more directional influence over economic affairs. It is rather because there can be no profitable business, large or small, which does not respond to its ultimate constituency, the buying public.

CHAPTER IV

Of the farm revolution

"For Antonia and for me, this had been the road of destiny."

—WILLA CATHER, *My Antonia*

AMONG THE PROFITS and losses of this age of industrial expansion must be counted those inherent in jet transportation, by which the span of a continent has been contracted to less than six hours. Granted that the pressurized cabin affords an indispensable convenience to the executive, who can close a deal in San Francisco on the same day his attorneys draw up the papers in New York, and to the labor leader who, breakfasting in his split-level home on the outskirts of Detroit, can turn up that noon in the cloakrooms of Congress. Yet just as certainly something has been lost along the way—something which those who recall the wonders of clicking westward over the rails of the Union Pacific or the Santa Fe will cherish with more than nostalgia. However time-consuming a three-day-and-night passage across the American continent may be, it is at least a potent reminder of the land from which the seeds of industry have sprouted. Even Premier Khrushchev, not so bright in many ways, got the point on his visit here in 1959. Having paid his disrespect to the White House and pounded his shoe in the United Nations, he headed for the tall corn of Iowa.

For the corn is there in abundance, and beyond it the wheat, and almost everywhere the grazing cattle. And without them there would, of course, be no Cleveland, Dayton, Indianapolis, or Denver—or the executive sitting behind his desk in Rockefeller Center, figuring his next move in Saudi Arabia. On the land this age of affluence began, and if one has an eye for statistics one still realizes that agriculture is not only America's basic industry, but palpably an enormous one, including 8.5 million square miles of the good earth and a total investment in land, buildings, livestock, and machinery running to some $194 billion. Agriculture is likewise one of America's most diversified and efficient industries, with results that are both disconcerting and hopeful. At the birth of the Republic it is estimated that some 90 per cent of all Americans lived from the land, and could be counted as sons and daughters of the soil. Today the figure is down to less than 8 per cent and is still decreasing, and even this does not tell the whole story of what is taking place. By Census Bureau definition, there are still some 3,700,000 farms scattered across the U.S., some large, some medium-sized, some

smaller than ten acres. The great business of feeding
and helping clothe America, however, is carried on
by no more than 2,000,000 farms which produce
nearly 90 per cent of the corn, wheat, cotton, fruits,
vegetables, milk, pork, and beef sold at market,
stored away in bursting granaries, or given away to
succor the less fortunate nations of the world.

This ability of so few to contribute so much to so
many has been heralded in many quarters as the
great American farm "problem," but it is a problem
in which Soviet Russia, which still has to devote
some 50 per cent of its manpower resources to the
land, would gladly share, as would all other underdeveloped nations. For historically, of course, it is
the release of men and women from the soil and the
hard business of eking out a bare subsistence which
has allowed civilization to flower. Were the American
farmer still that engaging "Jack-of-all-trades" he was a
century ago, we might in some ways have a pleasanter
country, but at forfeit of most of the independent
trades, industry, and commerce which have developed
on the base of a more efficient agriculture. It has been
precisely this efficiency which has allowed the staffing
of our factories, mills, oil refineries, and defense establishments, without which there would be no United
States as we know it. What has been going on, in
the trenchant phrase of Karl Brandt of the Food
Research Institute, is a "piecemeal disassembling
and reassembling" of the economy, wherein employment on the land has been diminishing while non-

farm employment has been rapidly increasing, shooting up from 38 million to 61 million in the two decades between 1940 and 1960.

In such perspective the farm story, so often told in sorrow and in anger, is as brilliant a saga of economic development and increasing division of labor as has ever been written by free men on the face of this planet—a saga no less instructive because it dramatizes the close interconnection between agriculture and industrial business. The initial strength of the American farm community rested in the courage and versatility of the men and women who, having colonized the Eastern Seaboard, pushed across the Alleghenies, cleared the rich bottom land of the mid-continent, survived the heat and the cold of the Great Plains, twisted through the Rockies and the Sierras, and arrived at last at the fertile edge of the Pacific.

The reinforcing strength of this movement came from the industrial revolution and the factories which sprouted almost as fast as the corn and wheat the farmer planted. Without Eli Whitney's cotton gin there never would have been a splendid South. The McCormick reaper made the oceans of grain possible. The perfection of the internal combustion engine and the rise of the automobile industry extended the farmer's mobility, first provided by the railroads, and put at his command a multimillion form of horsepower in the tractor and powered combine. The rise of the chemical industry and the magic application of nitrogen (shooting up from less than 500,000 tons in the pre-World War II era to over 3,000,000 tons per year today) have increased per acre yield beyond belief. It is the combination of all these things which allows each American farmer today to produce enough food and fibers for himself and twenty-eight others, whereas a Soviet farmer can produce only enough for himself and four others. As a result, after forty years of brutal collectivization, Russia must turn to the West for the staff of life.

2.

In view of the record it is ironic, to say the least, that our history books devote so much time, on the one hand, to detailing the farmer's grievances against industry and, on the other, to playing up the alleged virtues of lavish government programs for settling the score. On the first point, it was no doubt natural for the farmer to view with a certain amount of suspicion the smoking chimneys which rose at his back as he domesticated a continent, to distrust the hard-money men of Wall Street from whom he had to borrow, and to look with disfavor on the railroad magnate who had the inside track in the setting of freight rates. Yet again, in broader perspective, the basic troubles of the farmer in our time cannot be put down to the rise of the great corporation but go back to general causes. The upward sweep of farm

prices and profits in World War I sowed the seeds of
painful readjustment of the 'twenties and 'thirties.
The great depression itself was a national tragedy in
which the downward plunge of industrial production pulled down farm prices and incomes, which in
their turn contributed to the deflationary spiral. If
we assume war as a norm, then American agriculture
will always be on a spree. If we assume depression as
a norm, with widespread urban unemployment, then
indeed the farmer will always need help, as will almost everybody else.

Yet these are palpably defeatist assumptions for
framing long-term policy, which should aim at stabilizing the economy through general credit and
fiscal measures while enlarging, rather than constricting, the scope of the market for all producers,
whether they be industrial concerns or farmers. Unhappily, modern farm legislation from the New Deal
forward has lurched off in the opposite direction,
seeking to prop up agricultural prices by artificial
means in the vain pursuit of a mythical "parity"
standard based on obsolete and unattainable norms.
The result of tinkering with prices has jammed the
vital signaling system which relays to producers what
the consumer wants and can pay for, and has given
rise to mounting surpluses which are a clear waste of
resources, not to mention the taxpayer's money.

In the 'sixties, the government has been paying
out between $5 and $6 billion per year to agriculture,
with the largest portion of this money going to price

support operations. For its pains, the U.S. now holds some $7.2 billion in wheat, cotton, corn, and other commodities, with storage charges alone running to some $500 million per year. These surpluses represent an increasing threat to the very prices the government is seeking to support, as well as a source of mounting worry to farmers themselves, who today as never before are conscious of the criticism of city-dwellers who pay the taxes for the government's folly. In the corn belt, the shimmering aluminum-painted storage bins, and, in the wheat belt, the tall concrete eleva-tors stuffed with surplus are an eyesore on an other-wise beautiful landscape. "We must get rid of them somehow," ruminated a wheat farmer recently, "if we are to hold our heads up."

But how? The facile and dangerous answer is ever stricter controls over production, which from the first have been part of price-support schemes. These controls involve acreage allotments, under which farmers must hold down production on acres planted to certain norms in order to enjoy the benefits of price supports, and still harsher marketing quotas, by which farmers are penalized for not going along with the program. The dangers and difficulties here are proverbial. Faced with restricted allotments, farmers simply pour more fertilizer onto the acres they are allowed, thus easily defeating the con-trollers. In a single decade, for instance, output of wheat per acre in the wheat belt has risen from 17.3 bushels to 25.5 bushels, and the new de Kalb hybrid promises a still further increase. Moreover, as acres are cut down in one commodity, operators naturally turn to another. Restriction of wheat and cotton acreage over the years has led to increased production of corn and other feed grains. Hence these also have been brought under the allotment scheme. Yet efforts to control corn output in particular are beset with extraordinary difficulties, since almost any farmer can grow it in most states of the union and use it for feeding hogs and cattle. "All that Washington has been doing," complains a corn belt farmer, "is to chase the acres around."

Stringent controls have long been the rule in tobacco growing, where they have "worked" after a fashion, owing to peculiarities in the market—the confinement of flue-cured tobacco to a relatively small area and the presence of a few large buyers, the big tobacco companies. Even so, the arrangement, amounting to a cartel, has had its costs—the distortion of the price of land, which all too often sells on the basis of its allotment, and the elimination from the market of many small, indigent farmers, who have as much abstract right to grow tobacco as the favored few. In cotton, where allotments and marketing quotas have also long ruled, the costs have been still heavier. Artificial prices for King Cotton have meant increasing competition from domestic synthetics. In addition, commercial cotton exports, which in the 'twenties ran to some 7,500,000 bales per year, have suffered drastically. Exports are now highly dependent on government giveaway programs and export subsidy schemes which have run into their own peculiar troubles. Foreign producers of textiles buy U.S. cotton at cheaper prices than domestic producers and promptly invade U.S. markets. And so there is constant pressure for higher tariffs and quotas on textile imports; and it is proposed that domestic manufacturers get their cotton at a special discount from the government. Thus one subsidy leads on to another in a fantastic way, with the forgotten consumer, of course, footing the bill.

In the face of these difficulties with price supports and controls, it is all but incredible that men of sound mind can seriously propose more of the same. Yet, in fact, such a proposal was the essence of the so-called "new approach" to agriculture trumpeted by the Kennedy administration in 1960. Under this approach, farm prices would be jacked up still higher, in return for stricter marketing controls over an increasing number of commodities. Stripped of its niceties, the program would have sought to impose on the bulk of the farm economy a kind of *cartel* arrangement which the government opposes in the case of industry. It would also have given the government powers which, as Henry Wallace noted, would be as onerous as any possessed by the Soviet Union. In the first decisive test of this actually very old approach, wheat farmers voted the proposal down by a clear majority. They could, of course, in the future change their minds, but their original instinct was surely

sound. Government-controlled cartelization is no answer to the problems of the farm economy. Rather,
strict control over farm output must in the end lead to
control over input if it is to be effective. In its agricultural program the New Frontier was in fact bidding
for total economic planning that, beginning on the
farm, could infect and stultify the entire competitive
market system.

3.

Yet, quite aside from these larger considerations,
such planning is highly unsuited to the complexities
of agriculture, which has tended to make obsolete
and a bit ridiculous the whole apparatus of price
supports and controls so laboriously erected. In past
and present farm legislation, Congressmen continue
to talk of the nation's six "basic" crops, by which
they mean wheat, cotton, tobacco, corn, rice, and
peanuts. But a fertile and generous continent produces not six, but literally hundreds of farm products, including lespedeza, pecans, artichokes, garlic,
mint, shallots, avocados, rabbits, pigeons, and guinea
hens, not to mention silver fox and mink! And even
if we talk seriously of "basic" products, it has long
been recognized that the priorities given in most
farm programs have little relevance to actual economic facts. In order of magnitude, the great cash
crops of 1962, to choose a single year, broke down as
follows:

Meat animals (largely hogs and cattle)	$11.8 billion
Dairy products	4.8 billion
Poultry, eggs	3.1 billion
Cotton (lint and seed)	2.6 billion
Wheat	2.1 billion
Vegetables	1.9 billion
Corn	1.8 billion
Fruits and nuts	1.6 billion
Soya beans	1.5 billion
Tobacco	1.3 billion

The breakdown is interesting in more ways than one. At least two of the so-called "basic" crops, peanuts and rice, do not even rank among major money crops. On the other hand vegetables and fruits, which enjoy little or no support, are flourishing; and the truck farmer, while not always the happy warrior, is perhaps the best answer to those who argue that if the government withholds aid the whole farm economy will collapse. More significant still is the importance of meat products, which have been steadily rising as personal incomes and hence demand for protein foods increase. These likewise enjoy no direct government price support though it can be argued that propping up corn prices indirectly supports the price of hogs; and for this reason many midwest corn-hog producers still favor some kind of feed crop support. Yet, in the long run, higher prices for feed crops also increase the *cost* of hogs, reducing profit margins and constricting the ultimate market for pork, which is by no means inelastic. The same point applies with even more force to the market for beef, where the housewife surely does vary her buying according to price. The oft-repeated allegation that agriculture is a "special case" because lower prices cannot greatly increase demand is doubtful, even in the case of wheat and tobacco if export markets are counted. It is surely untrue in the case of beef, which is the most flourishing and most rapidly expanding sector of the entire farm economy.

Indeed, the hope of farm prosperity in the future depends uniquely, in the opinion of many experts, on a continuing shift away from old, tired, over-supported crops and into a still larger output of meat products. More generally, it lies in further mechanization and diversification, which have already gone far and fast. The visitor to western Kansas, which was once overcommitted to wheat, is surprised to find cattle coming up, not from Texas, but from Georgia and Mississippi, once wholly committed to King Cotton. The Coachella Valley in California, north of the Salton Sea, is still the date capital of America, but because of irrigation from the Colorado River, it is now able to diversify into low-cost cotton and vegetables—onions and carrots—raised on forty and sixty-acre plots. All over the broad land there is hopeful movement and the display of twentieth-century ingenuity, which, differing from that of the pioneers, is no less important and dramatic. A new breed of farmer is coming into prominence—men educated in the intricacies of modern production and willing to take their chances in the market place. "I am committed to farming," said a young California operator recently, "but I am also committed to making it pay. If it doesn't pay out, I shouldn't be in it and I won't be."

It should be the aim of government policy to capitalize upon rather than to thwart these new and hopeful trends by progressively *lowering* price supports on protected crops and unwinding the whole apparatus of controls, which has proved itself a mounting burden and danger. When all is said and done, there is no other way to solve the farm "problem," which is a mystery only to those who will not look facts in the face. In progressively lowering supports, the government would have large responsibility for holding existing surpluses off the market for a considerable period, recognizing that a quarter-century of mischief cannot be undone overnight. Yet a beginning must be made and made now, in the interest of farmer and taxpayer alike, to get the government out of the agricultural business, and there is evidence that this can and should be done without incurring a general collapse of farm prices, and without prejudice to those farmers who may need assistance during the transition.

4.

For among all the other defects of the present system, none is more remarkable than that most government price support operations primarily benefit large commercial farmers rather than those at the bottom of the income scale. Here the Census Bureau figures have given rise to great rivers of confusion, though if properly interpreted they are highly revealing. By Census definition, a farm is a place of ten acres, or more, selling $50 or more of produce yearly, or even a still smaller unit if it produces (as do some tobacco plots) $250 or more of produce. Such definition obviously includes a lot of diverse territory, both geographic and human. Thus of the 3,700,000 "farms" in the U.S., as defined by the Bureau, nearly 1,000,000 are operated on a part-time basis, and some 400,000 are lived on by people in retirement with outside sources of income. Commercial farms number some 2,500,000, ranging from those which sell as little as $50 in the market to big operators at the top selling $40,000 or more. The lower tiers of these commercial farms are undoubtedly poor, but the upper tiers are relatively affluent. They include the Texas cattle rancher who may own 75,000 acres and may net $250,000 per year, the Kansas wheat farmer who also goes in for large acreage, the large dairy farmer of Wisconsin and the Northeast, and the plain ordinary farmer, found in most of the fifty-one states, who goes in for some dairying, some corn, some hogs, with vegetables and poultry as side lines.

It is patently absurd and, indeed, unjust to overlook this diversity and to spend some $5 billion per year on a price-support system under which the more successful a farmer becomes the more he receives from his government. It is likewise not very sensible to try through government subsidies to restore a parity relationship between farm and non-farm income. On the basis of somewhat arcane calculations, the Department of Agriculture estimates that the per capita income of the entire present farm population, in so far as it is derived from farming, runs around $950, as against a per capita income for the non-farm population of some $2,450—indeed a large gap. When outside sources of income are added, however, the farm figure rises to $1,450—indicating that a large number of people now counted as farmers have outside jobs, a healthy phenomenon. But this is not all. The differential between per capita farm income from all sources and per capita non-farm income rests in large measure on the liberality of the Census Bureau in its definition of what constitutes a farm and farmer. Revise that definition to include only those who are actually in the farming business and the farm income figure would of course rise, though the problem of poverty would remain.

The point is that we should distinguish sharply between the problems inherent in agriculture itself and the broader problem of poverty, which is present throughout our affluent society. In doing so, we should discontinue large government payments to those who do not need them in order to have more left over for those who do. The historic trek from the land to the city which has been going on for generations has not been due to the fact that some evil genius has *forced* people off the land, but rather to the fact that men and women saw a better chance for themselves in migrating to where incomes were higher. We should not seek to interrupt this trend, in so far as it is necessary. On the other hand, we should not fall prey to the cruel fallacy that people will necessarily gain by swapping the poverty of the southern delta for the poverty of city slums. Many of the agricultural poor will be better off living where they are while increasing their earnings by part-time employment in industry. The most hopeful single statistic in the great maze of farm statistics is that today those who live on the land *receive some $7 billion from non-farm sources, as against $13 billion from strictly agricultural operations*. Such outside income is likely to increase rather than to diminish as industry proliferates and decentralizes.

This is only to stress that the problems of U.S. agriculture, no less than its fabulous achievements, are inextricably linked with those of industry, and cannot be segregated or compartmentalized. For the years ahead, the proper balance of agricultural and industrial resources cannot be figured out by officials sitting in Washington with their slide rules. For they too, *mirabile dictu,* are fallible human beings, and so have no superior knowledge of what specific farm prices and farm population should be in the world of tomorrow. The need is rather to keep our society fluid and open-ended, allowing the market process to do its work in the interest of efficiency and freedom while at the same time alleviating real distress where it is present. But if this is to be our guide in agricultural matters, we must also see to it that it is our guide in other departments of the American experiment. If farm prices are to be fluid and not fixed, so should industrial wages and the industrial process. The interests of the farmer and the industrial worker and the businessman, so often juxtaposed in opposition to each other, have a broad identity at this deeper level. It is time we turned back from the broad land to the factories which an efficient agriculture has made possible—to the problems of industrial employment and of over-all economic stability and growth.

CHAPTER V

Of wages and labor unions

"The theory of wages as elaborated in this book has not proved a cheerful subject."

—J. R. HICKS, *The Theory of Wages*

IN THE EPIC TRANSFORMATION of America from a predominantly rural to an industrialized society, we have emphasized a vast and beneficent increase in agricultural production accompanied by a decline in the number of those contributing to it. This is because agriculture, however basic to our society, constitutes only one segment or department of the economic process. When we open the lens wider and survey that process as a whole, we discover a still more dramatic panorama. From the early nineteenth century forward, industrial production has greatly expanded, accompanied by a vast increase in non-agricultural employment to well over sixty million workers. This expansion absorbed the great trek of men and women from the land to the city, as well as a vast inpouring of immigrants—Irish, Italian, German, Czech, and Lithuanian. It is this immigration which has given American democracy its precious multi-racial heritage, and which still makes the aging statue at the entrance to New York Harbor a meaningful symbol, even though now the gates have narrowed. Once more, no one planned it that way. The New World, celebrated in the haunting theme of Dvořák's Fifth Symphony, held out its arms, and the peddlers and the puddlers and the incipient skilled carpenters and machinists responded to the promise of greater opportunity ahead.

On the whole they found that opportunity, despite many a disappointment and heartbreak. Indeed, so far America has proved to be the practical refutation of Malthus' gloomy thesis that increase in population and in those seeking work must inevitably spread poverty. The history of the American worker, though, as in the case of the farmer, containing many a painful passage, is likewise one of extraordinary achievement. In the century of advance between 1850 and 1950, it is estimated that real hourly wages of the ordinary worker rose at least fourfold, and have continued to climb. Weekly and annual earnings have advanced somewhat less rapidly as the result of the progressive reduction of working hours and the shortening of the work week. This is only to say, however, that the capitalist market economy has not only succeeded in increasing measurable incomes, which are today the envy of the outside world, but has likewise led to an increase in intangible satisfactions, including more leisure.

This double advance in both wages and living standards has sometimes been attributed to the rise of unionism which, starting as a reaction to the factory system, has come to play a dominant role in our society. Yet whatever the contribution of unionism to the social status of the American worker, it cannot be regarded as the prime mover in the progress which palpably stretches all around us. Real wages in this country began to rise long before powerful unions became intrenched in the basic industries, and the proportion of industrial income going for wages as against the fraction going for profits and other elements of the national income has held fairly constant over the long pull. The alleged conflict between labor and capital conceals the deeper affinity which binds them together. The true engine of economic advance has been industry's creative investment in better tools and machines, which in increasing man-hour productivity per worker has released resources to satisfy new human demands and has led on to the expansion of markets.

The critical question for maintaining such expansion involves the nature of this connection between employer and worker, and what determines the relationship. On this point government economists, not to mention labor leaders and politicians, have of late had little doubt. Working with statistics

which all too often overmagnify the extent of unemployment in the U.S.,[1] the new economic orthodoxy stresses the maintenance of so-called "aggregate
demand" or purchasing power in the economy
through government fiscal and credit policies. Let
the government spend more money, runs the argument, and business will soon enough be creating
jobs for all who are, in the language of the Employment Act of 1946, "able, willing, and seeking to
work." Thereafter let government so arrange things
that the economy "grows" at a certain percentum per
year, and full or nearly full employment as well as
increasing welfare will be guaranteed in perpetuity.

Now it cannot be doubted that monetary policy in
its broadest sense can have an important role to play
in helping to maintain the economy at high employment and production levels—a point to be examined
in detail in subsequent chapters. Sufficient to stress
here that the new orthodoxy of government spending
cannot explain past economic development, where
government played a far smaller role in the economy
than it does today. Long before modern economists
came on the scene to tell us that all will be well if
the federal treasury keeps the economy humming,
employers and employees had found a mutually
profitable means of getting together. The means
obviously was and still is the price and profit system,
of which wages are an essential part. Without a grasp
of traditional wage theory we are not likely to devise

[1] See Appendix I, Note on Employment Statistics.

proper policies for maintaining both over-all employment and continuous, humane advance.

2.

Let us remind ourselves more precisely of what the "traditional wisdom" in these matters actually entails. Fundamentally it held and holds that wage rates are a form of price, whose function in adjusting demand and supply for particular grades of work is not too different from that of other prices. This traditional view of wage determination seems to clash head on with the often-repeated dictum that "labor is not a commodity." Of course, it is not if by labor we mean human beings. But a man's work and talents, as distinguished from his person, certainly are commodities, indeed the most precious he possesses; and if a man is to preserve his freedom it is absolutely essential that he be able to sell his abilities and skills in the market place without let or hindrance. When this freedom is curtailed or annulled—when the government takes on the job of "allocating" human resources—the result is a kind of slavery. Indeed, it is precisely in Communist countries, where everything is centrally planned, that human beings are treated as commodities. Far from being an inhumane theory, the market view of wage determination is the only one consonant with human liberty and dignity.

If wages are prices, then within limits they will, or should, behave like other prices. Where demand for, say, carpenters is high, the wages of carpenters will rise, and vice versa. But it also follows that if the wages of carpenters are artificially boosted, there will be a curtailment of demand for their work. Technically expressed, the wage of any particular kind of labor under competitive conditions will tend to equal what economists call its "marginal product" or worth. If wages are below that level, there will be an insufficient supply of the class of labor in question, and employers will tend to bid up the wage rate. But if wages are set above that figure, there will be a falloff in demand for labor.

This truth has been questioned, especially by labor leaders, who insist that wage increases must be good because they increase "purchasing power." But this does not necessarily follow. The confusion here arises from not distinguishing between wage rates and total payrolls. For instance, if a firm is employing twenty men at $2 an hour, but would employ twenty-five men at $1.90 per hour, payrolls and purchasing power would advance if wage rates fell. On the other hand, if a firm is employing twenty men at $2 per hour and wages rise to $2.25, it may be forced to cut back employment to only fifteen men. In this case, purchasing power has actually dropped, even though wage rates have advanced. The wage rate is only part of the equation; what makes for purchasing power is payroll.

It is often argued, of course, that traditional wage analysis is purely "theoretical," and lacks statistical proof. It is all very well, say the critics, to say that artificial wage rates have an "unemployment effect," but where are the facts to back up the statement? It should be noted that those who ask this question rarely apply it to other sectors of the economy. For example, no one questions the proposition that high business prices can restrict demand in most circumstances. In the matter of interest rates, too, New Dealers and New Frontiersmen have been confident that high interest rates restrict demand for capital, while low interest rates stimulate borrowing. Yet if they were asked to prove this empirically they would be hard put to do it (especially since high interest rates are often the accompaniment of boom, and low interest rates of recession). The fact is that "proof" in economics is difficult because economics deals with human beings and precludes what scientists call a "controlled" experiment.

Nevertheless, there does exist a considerable body of evidence that maladjustments in wage rates are one, if not *the* most important, cause of unemployment. Nor is this proposition upheld only by economists living in the Dark Ages. In the 1920's, the brilliant Frenchman Jacques Rueff conducted a study of British unemployment and came to the conclusion that rigidity in the British wage structure was one of its critical causes. Rueff's work was reinforced by Josiah Stamp, by the British economist Arthur Pigou, and, surprisingly, by the late Lord Beveridge, who in his book, *Full Employment in a Free Society*,[2] states flatly: "As a matter of theory, the continuance in any country of a substantial vol-

2 (New York: George Allen & Unwin, 1944).

ume of unemployment . . . is in itself proof that the price being asked for labor as wages is too high for the conditions of the market; demand for and supply of labor are not finding the appropriate price of meeting."

In the United States, the importance of proper wage adjustment in determining employment was powerfully emphasized by the late Sumner Slichter, coiner of the term "the laboristic society," and by Senator Paul H. Douglas of Illinois before he took to the political hustings. In his monumental book, *The Theory of Wages*,[3] Douglas argues that the demand for labor is highly "elastic," meaning that a small change in the wage rate can have far-reaching consequences. Indeed, he states that if wages are pushed only 1 per cent above the point of marginal productivity—or, in plain language, the market worth of labor—the result might be a 3 to 4 per cent decline in employment.

But perhaps the most surprising witness in this respect is the late John Maynard Keynes, whose name is generally associated with the notion that rising wages must inevitably create more purchasing power. Those who interpret him this way without qualification have presumably not read his books. In *The General Theory of Employment, Interest and Money*,[4] probably the most influential single economic text of our time, Keynes states that he has no

3 (New York: Augustus M. Kelley, 1957).
4 (New York: Harcourt, Brace & World, Inc., 1936).

quarrel with the classical theory that if wages are boosted above marginal product unemployment will result. He goes on to say: *"With a given organization, equipment, and technique, real wages and the volume of output (and hence of employment) are uniquely correlated, so that, in general, an increase in employment can only occur to the accompaniment of a decline in the rate of real wages."*

This is, to say the least, a startling statement, considering how often Keynes' name has been invoked to justify wage increases as generating prosperity. In fact, he said something quite different. For political as well as economic reasons, Keynes did not believe in the over-all *cutting* of money wages as a recession cure. He did believe that government spending might reflate the economy under certain conditions. But the whole point of such spending was to raise prices *faster* than wages, and so restore business profits and investment. If, however, wages advanced with prices, or if prices were frozen while wages advanced, then under the conditions posited by Keynes the hoped-for result of government spending would be aborted. Profits would not recover and employment would not expand. Something like this seems to have happened in the 'thirties when, despite considerable government spending, the New Deal never conquered the unemployment problem. There were some 12,000,000 unemployed when Mr. Roosevelt took office, and there were still 8,000,000 unemployed in 1940, when the coming of war finally put men back to work. It is a notable fact that in this period wages rose very rapidly. Between 1932 and 1940, indeed, money wages in manufacturing advanced by 48 per cent and real wages rose by 44 per cent! This, according to Keynes' own reasoning, would have been enough partially to explain the great prolongation of the depression.

3.

Does all this mean that Keynes and other economists are hard-hearted men who believe that wages can never rise? Of course not. Over any period of time, industrial techniques are not frozen, as the Keynesian model assumes, and new inventions are constantly developed which tend to raise man-hour productivity and hence the market worth of, and the demand for, labor. But it matters profoundly how wage advances are timed and how technological advance is handled. By and large, the worst of all times to raise wage rates is during recession, when human resources are already unemployed. More generally, the benefits of technological advance in an industry will be most smoothly achieved if the advance is accompanied by *price* reductions in the industry in question, thus releasing consumer purchasing power for the purchase of other goods and services and the general expansion of markets. Henry Ford's Model T automobile obsoleted the carriage trade to the great discomfort of both its employers and employees. But, partly through reduction in price, the Model T ushered in a whole new industrial age which provided far more employment than had been taken away, both in Detroit and throughout the country, in a host of subsidiary industries. In the last analysis, technology not only stimulates total output, but helps create and maintain the demand for that output.

But this whole process of absorption of new techniques into the economic process may be fatally hampered and distorted through misguided wage policy. The bituminous coal industry, where today unemployment and misery is widespread, is a striking case in point. After World War II there were some 425,000 men employed in the soft coal industry. Thereafter, under union pressure, wages were pushed up rapidly with no great gain in productivity, while at the same time the industry was subjected to rising competition from oil and natural gas. Caught in a squeeze between prices and rising costs, operators turned dramatically to mechanization of the mines, substituting machines for men, and by 1961 employment had been reduced to 137,000—with higher wages for those who had work, but poverty and disaster threatening those thrown out of jobs. In 1952, when bituminous coal wages in Illinois were around $2.29 per hour, it did not pay to buy a machine at an annual cost of $2,500, even though it could save 1,000 man hours of work per year. With wage rates in 1961 at \$3.29 per hour, plus huge fringe benefits, the same machine did pay off, though its annual cost had risen to \$3,000.

To men turned away from the mines of West Virginia and eastern Kentucky—two of the country's worst depressed areas—it must appear that mechanization is the villain of the piece. The actual moral is something rather different. It is that where mechanization is pressed forward simply as an embattled response to wage advances already made or in the making, and where these advances, so to speak, "chew up" all productivity gains, the social dislocations of technology are bound to be severe. Where, on the other hand, wage advances follow rather than outpace mechanization, and where the benefits of such progress are widely shared, the results are far more humane.

This distinction is worth stressing at a time when it is being said that "automation" is a curse to our society rather than a blessing, representing a complete and revolutionary break with the past. The break is more apparent than real. In the new lexicon, experts have coined the word "cybernetic," derived from the Greek word for steersman, to describe machines which guide other machines or attend to themselves without manual help. But the homely thermostat is an instrument which guides another machine—the furnace—yet it would be foolish to argue that its invention has caused widespread unemployment. Quite the reverse is true.

The underlying truth is that in a world of automation and computers we need as never before a flexible wage and price system, to "steer" the course of invention. In a dynamic economy, where such invention is proceeding apace, we may expect that real wages will advance in the long run, with an over-all productivity gain of, say, 2 per cent per year, either through a gentle fall in the price level or a gentle rise in money wages. But this expectation should not be taken to mean that such advance should go forward under conditions of less than maximum practical employment, or that each industry or firm should be expected to pass all of its productivity advance on to its employees. On the contrary, as economist Fritz Machlup has argued with great force,[5] it is essential that the high technology industries be free to pass on part of *their* productivity gain to the public in the form of price reduction. In doing so they will expand their own markets and, more importantly, the consumer will find that he has more money to spend on other products. The result will be to expand rather than to contract over-all demand and employment.

4.

The greatest contribution which government can make to this wage-price process is not in inventing elaborate productivity "guidelines," but rather in

[5] *Review of Economics and Statistics* (May, 1960).

seeing that roadblocks do not clutter up the broad highway of advance. Unfortunately, government labor policy, like its agricultural policy, has all too often tended to press in a different direction, both directly and by encouragement of strong union pressures. In specifying certain conditions of work, in eliminating child labor, and through various factory legislation, government has played a useful and humane role. Much less can be said for its attempt to put minimum floors under wages which all too often tend to penalize those who are in greatest need— those workers at the bottom of the social scale.

The boosting of minimum wages in 1950 to 75 cents per hour, for example, caused a sharp drop in employment in southern sawmills.[6] When the rate was again boosted to $1 per hour in 1956, it caused a large displacement of workers in many of the poorer counties of Florida, as well as a general fall in employment among teen-age and elderly workers.[7] When the Kennedy administration came to office in 1961, one of its first moves was again to boost minimum wages to $1.25 per hour, causing adverse effects on the very unemployment it was setting out to cure. The original framers of the minimum wage law were quite conscious of its dangers. The Fair Labor Standards Act of 1938 specifically states that wage floors should not be raised to a point that would jeopardize job opportunities. In thus framing the law, its spon-

[6] John M. Petersen, *Journal of Political Economy* (October, 1957).
[7] Marshall R. Colberg, *Journal of Law and Economics* (October, 1960).

sors showed themselves more astute students of economics than many modern-day liberals who argue that raising minimum wage standards under any and all conditions is a step ahead for the country.

Far more important and controversial has been the effect on wages and employment exercised by trade unions which government policy has done so much to foster. It is elementary that in the long run union organization of and by itself cannot raise the *real* wages of *all* workers in the community, since this rise depends fundamentally on capital investment. What unions are able to do is something quite different—namely, to raise *money* wages for *particular groups* within the working class higher than they otherwise might have been for temporary and sometimes for fairly long periods. Even their influence in this narrower field is subject to considerable debate among economists. One minimal estimate is that union action has raised money wages by about 15 per cent for some 10 per cent of the labor force. Others would put these figures much higher, but in any case it is not the general over-all percentage that counts. What counts is the fact that in particular industries, notably in the bituminous coal industry, already examined, unions have been able to push up wage rates to extravagant figures in the very teeth of widespread unemployment. The high rates of pay in the building trades are undoubtedly partly attributable to union action, not just at the bargaining table but through their ability to restrict "freedom of entry" for new workers coming into these trades. The relatively high wages of truck drivers cannot easily be explained by shortage of men able and willing to barrel trucks down the nation's highways. To no inconsiderable extent they are the result of the power of the Teamster's Union, which Mr. Hoffa built into a nationwide institution with ambitious plans for dominating all forms of transportation.

To respectable, well-meaning union leaders who see organization as the means for furthering the "cause" of labor, all this is reason for considerable satisfaction. The economist and the plain ordinary citizen must see the case somewhat differently. In exceptional cases, where business firms enjoy a clearcut monopoly position in the matter of hiring, wages may be pressed down below the level where competition would put them, and unionization may play a useful economic role in redressing the balance. But to the degree that, in the presence of widespread industry and intra-industry competition, unions succeed in driving and holding wages above market levels, the results must be to constrict rather than to enlarge employment opportunities, as all our previous analysis has shown.

Nor are the adverse results confined to the specific firm or industry in question; rather they spread far and wide. Excessive wages in steel or automobiles, while benefiting those who have jobs, tend to reduce mobility and job opportunities for other sections of the work force, and are particularly hard on the unskilled worker at the bottom of the social ladder. The employer who might pay $1.50 per hour for a Negro sweeper in a Detroit factory may employ no sweepers at all if the wage were forced to, say, $2. The bunching of unemployment in recent years among Negroes, the unskilled, and "drop-outs" from high school—so often deplored by the Department of Labor—is commonly attributed only to mechanization, and it is popular to argue that it can only be cured through special retraining and educational programs. Such programs are indeed needed, but in the meantime it is safe to say that many unskilled workers might well find useful employment if wages in the heavily organized industries were lower, more flexible, and responsive to basic supply and demand conditions.

Put bluntly, all this means that the straight economic gains of unionism have been much overrated, and that in so far as they occur they are almost always achieved at the expense of other workers. As the late Henry Simons put it a good many years ago: "The semblance of struggle between labor and capital conceals the substantial conflict between . . . established workers in more remunerative occupations and workers elsewhere. The masses of the unorganized and unorganizable lose as consumers; they lose by being denied access to higher wage areas; and they lose by an artificial abundance of labor in the markets where they must sell. . . . And let no one infer that their problem would be solved if they too were organized. The monopoly racket, like that of tariffs and subsidies, works only so long as it is exceptional— works only to advantage minorities relatively, with overall diseconomy and loss."[8]

This is a harsh saying but a true bill in so far as the economic consequences of big unions and industry-wide bargaining are concerned. But unions are obviously not just economic organizations. Their contribution to our society has been and should be social, alleviating injustice where it exists on the factory floor, mitigating the sense of loneliness and "not belonging" which huge industrial establishments have fostered, and giving workers the sense that they too have rights which cannot be denied. But what rights? Originally, unions came into being as benevolent associations or clubs in response to the rise of the factory system, and were today's unions truly free associations, their role in society would have a sound moral and political basis. The difficulty, of course, is that this is not the case. The untamed tiger in the eye of many a union organizer is coercion—coercion that expresses itself in multiple forms. Perversely, unions have continued to press for the "closed" or union shop or variants of the same, which force workers as the price of their jobs to contribute to labor organizations. The undoubted right of men to lay down their tools in order to better their condition has been perverted into the doctrine of not allowing

<hr/>

[8] *Economic Policy for a Free Society* (Chicago: University of Chicago Press, 1948).

others to take up those tools, on pain of subtle or open retaliation. Finally, just below the surface of collective bargaining, as now practiced, there runs a stream of violence, threatened or overt, which is by no means confined to the drab reaches of the New York or San Francisco waterfronts.

5.

In the face of these multiple challenges to the free and open society it is little wonder that many students of the labor movement, and not just die-hard businessmen, have counseled the need for reform. But what kind of reform? The popular view, continually voiced in periods of "crisis," as when the unions closed down the newspapers of New York, is that government should "do something" about the situation, interfering directly with the process of bargaining and bringing the contending parties to terms by force. This impulse, while perhaps natural, overlooks the patent danger of a further expansion of government power, and the further fact that the powers enjoyed by unions today are largely government-created.

The history of U.S. labor legislation is a long and complicated one, but leaves little doubt about this essential fact. Through the Clayton Act of 1914, labor unions were largely exempted from antitrust prosecution on the grounds, already examined, that the "labor of a human being is not a commodity." The

Norris-La Guardia Act of 1932 pushed this doctrine much further, largely exempting unions from temporary injunctive process in the federal courts and stressing the idea that labor disputes require special treatment under the law. Under the Wagner Act of 1935, the government went out of its way to encourage collective bargaining; made it mandatory that when a union wins a representative election, even by the barest majority, it becomes the sole bargaining agency for the entire group of workers involved; and set up the National Labor Relations Board as a new instrument for administering labor law. The Taft-Hartley Act of 1947 did something to redress the balance by specifying that employees shall be free to participate or *not* to participate in union activities, and by listing unfair union, as well as employer, practices. Yet Taft-Hartley, at first declared to be a "slave" labor law, made little dent in either labor union power or its corruptions, which struck the public full force in the famous McClellan Committee investigation of the late 'fifties. In the wake of that investigation, Congress passed the Landrum-Griffin Act, which sought to tighten up restrictions on secondary boycotts and certain forms of picketing, as well as to impose certain responsibilities and accountability on the part of union treasuries.

Yet today the authors of Landrum-Griffin are themselves disillusioned by the little it has accomplished, and it is fair to say that existing legislation

leaves firmly in place the exemptions and privileges
which make unions, legally speaking, unique in our
society. More basic reform would seek to strike down
those privileges, not by passing new federal legislation but by amending or repealing laws now on the
books. In the reform process we should insist on absolute "freedom of entry" into all trades and profes-
sions, as well as on the principle of voluntarism. The
provision in Taft-Hartley which allows the union
shop, under certain conditions, should be repealed,
and state *right-to-work* laws encouraged. It is sometimes argued that compulsory unionism is necessary
to prevent non-union workers from getting a "free
ride" on the backs of the organized. To this it must be
answered that it is the union which today enjoys a
free ride on the backs of other workers by insisting
that it must represent *all* the employees in a shop,
even if 49 per cent object. In addition, there is great
need for restoring due legal process in the enforcement of labor law. Professor Sylvester Petro of New
York University has argued powerfully for restoring
the use of temporary injunctions in labor disputes as
the only means of protecting employer and employee
from untold damage.[9] And Representative Landrum
recently introduced a bill in Congress which would
strip the National Labor Relations Board of its
powers to adjudicate labor disputes, and would return

9 *The Labor Policy of the Free Society* (New York: The Ronald Press
Company, 1957).

these in the first instance to the courts, thus limiting what has now become a no man's land of administrative law.

Congress should likewise reconsider whether unions should enjoy their wide exemption from the antitrust laws. The most frequent objection to this approach is that it would *smash* all unions, because by definition a union seeks to exercise monopoly power in bargaining for the sale of labor within its jurisdiction. But as Professor Patrick Boarman has pointed out in his book, *Union Monopolies and Antitrust Restraints*,[10] this is, to say the least, a purist view. A union bargaining for the workers of a particular plant or firm is a monopoly only if we argue that any association of individual men in a club, partnership, or business enterprise is a monopoly. What counts in defining monopoly, Boarman points out, is "the degree of market power" exercised by the business firm or union in question—its ability to control, not itself, but its external competitive environment. In many of our basic industries, unions today exert enormous power even though total union membership—estimated at about 17 million —tends to be declining absolutely and as a percentage of the total labor force. This power is not apt to "wither away" as in Marx's ill-founded dream of the state. Rather, if left unchecked it can hold adverse consequences for the free society. The U.S. is not apt to succumb to old-fashioned socialism, which has

[10] (Washington, D.C.: Labor Policy Association, Inc., 1963).

never held much attraction for the hard-headed American worker. But in a number of quarters it is urged that since nothing can be done about the size and power of unions we might as well accept a new situation, where Big Labor and Big Business will sit down together under government sponsorship and work out some kind of satisfactory arrangement about prices and wages. Yet the result of such collaboration is not apt to be happy, for the buying public or the preservation of competition. Indeed, we can see in this concept a kind of recrudescence of the New Deal's ill-conceived and ill-fated NRA, and beyond that the image of the corporate state.

Our need is not for more war, or for more "collaboration" between union and business, but rather for the enforcement of clear-cut rules governing both in the interest of the individual worker and the citizen consumer. From this point of view, the application of the spirit, if not the letter, of the Sherman Act would seem to have much to offer in restoring unionism to its proper role in our society. That role can be a great one: the protection of workers against the peculiar risks of their jobs; the continuance and, one trusts, the enlargement of benevolent functions of all kinds; and, in general, the civilizing of the industrial process. In performing such services, unions need no special privileges, and it is time that they stood on their own feet—the more so if they wish to appeal to the growing ranks of white collar workers. What is tolerably clear is that in exercising coercion

over their members unions strain the very principles
of the good society, and in pressing for excessive
wage rates they contribute to the general problem of
unemployment. It is fashionable to believe that such
unemployment can be cured and "floated off" by enlarged government spending and the magic of fiscal
and credit policies. But as will be shown in the next
chapter, such magic has its own peculiar and specific
limitations if we are to maintain the integrity of the
dollar, in which the wages of labor, no less than the
incomes of the rest of the community, are paid.

CHAPTER VI

Of money and spending

"Criticism surprises the soul in the arms of convention."
—GEORGE SANTAYANA, *Skepticism and Animal Faith*

THE POWERS OF THE FEDERAL GOVERNMENT
"to coin money [and] regulate the value thereof," no
less than its powers to tax and to spend, are constitu-
tionally grounded and fundamental. The question
that confronts each generation is how these broad
powers should be interpreted and used, and this has
in fact given rise to a continuous debate and contro-
versy since the founding of the Republic. Within
memory, the conventional wisdom on this subject
might be capsuled by saying that the government
should be committed to giving us a "sound" currency, and to paying its own bills on time. Today we
live in more sophisticated times, when governments
everywhere, and in the U.S. not least, seek to use
their broad monetary and fiscal powers to promote
high levels of output, employment, and growth.

This enlarged commitment may well hold the

promise that the U.S. need never again suffer the ravages of prolonged deflation, such as overtook the country in the depression 'thirties. It also poses its own inherent dangers. The economic danger is that in seeking to cure unemployment, which, as we have just seen, is frequently caused by trade union pressures, the government will propel us into a condition of more or less permanent inflation. The political danger, more ominous and more subtle, is that in seeking to "compensate" for every fluctuation in the private economy, the government will come to dominate the economy. We begin by conceding that the government has large responsibilities in the regulation of money creation and in properly arranging its now huge budgetary expenditures. We end, if we are not careful, with government becoming the grand manipulator and manager of our destinies.

2.

These dangers become more apparent when we remind ourselves of how easily the modern monetary system can be manipulated for good or ill by governmental agencies. The outstanding characteristic of the present system is the distance it has evolved from its original metallic base. Under the gold standard, to which the U.S. adhered until the early 'thirties, the U.S. dollar was fully convertible into gold both at home and abroad. Today gold is still used to settle

international balances, and the national gold stock—
now running to some $15.5 billion—determines the
ultimate assets of the country's twelve federal reserve
banks, and so may be said to be the underpinning for
the nation's currency and banking system. But gold
no longer circulates, and the reassuring gold piece no
longer turns up in the toe of the Christmas stocking.
The real business of the economy is transacted in
irredeemable paper money and, more importantly,
through checking accounts and bank deposits.

The rise of deposit money, which, of course, ante-
dated the demise of the gold standard, constitutes
one of the more baffling and surely one of the more
important inventions of man. For through it money
—defined as any acceptable means of payment—is
transmuted from something hard and tangible into
nothing more nor less than a human promise to meet
a personal signature. But, more, the modern deposit
system entails a peculiar magic whereby money is
multiplied in response to business *or* governmental
needs. The well-dressed conservative banker sitting
in his glass-enclosed office *seems* to be doing nothing
more than accepting a deposit of savings from customer A and lending part of the proceeds out at
interest to customer B. Yet this multiple lending
activity in fact expands deposits in the banking system
taken as a whole. See how the magic runs! At the end
of 1963 the total of currency in the hands of the public
—nickels, dimes, quarters, and folding bills—ran to
some $33 billion. But total demand deposits ran to

over $124 billion with $111 billion of commercial time deposits piled on top of that.

Now a system of this kind is not self-regulating and, as Walter Bagehot remarked long ago, "money will not manage itself." The fundamental instrument of regulation is the central bank, or, in the U.S., the Federal Reserve System, which is endowed with broad powers to expand or contract the "reserves" of member banks, and hence to encourage or to inhibit them from increasing their deposit liabilities. At the extreme, the Federal Reserve may actually change reserve requirements, which today run to about one-sixth of demand deposits. More subtly, the Fed can engage in so-called "open market" operations, which involve the purchase or sale of government obligations already issued as part of the national debt. In general, if the Federal Reserve buys up government obligations, it will increase commercial bank reserves and so tend to expand their lending activities. If it sells government obligations, it tends to decrease bank reserves and so tighten up on credit. Thus it turns out that the business of money creation, though partly in private hands, is responsive to government dictate through an art more complex and more important than that which the goldsmith of old exercised in stamping the head of the sovereign on a shimmering piece of metal.

Nor is this all. For while the Federal Reserve is a semi-autonomous agency, it cannot completely disregard what its neighbor, the Federal Treasury, is doing in the matter of managing the federal budget. If the Treasury is running a balanced budget, covering its immense outlays by taxes, its operations need not affect the money supply. If it is running a deficit, which is more likely nowadays, and chooses to sell high interest bonds to the investing public, it will again take in money about as fast as it spends it. But if the Treasury sells bonds into the banking system, somewhat different results follow. For in this case purchase of the bonds by the banks will tend to create deposits, much as if they had loaned out funds to business enterprises. This is a vast oversimplification of the process, but it drives home an important point.[1] The result of government spending depends to no small degree on how the spending is *financed*. And it is because modern governments have these large powers over money creation, as well as over taxing and spending, that they have such decisive influence on our economic fortunes.

3.

The critical problem, to repeat, is how and when these monetary and fiscal powers should be used and in what circumstances, and it is here that debate and argument begin. Up to the onset of the great depression in the 'thirties, it is fair to say that not only practical men of affairs but many economists

[1] See Appendix II, Note on Money.

had reached some agreement in these matters. In the first place there existed in those halcyon, if naïve, times more faith in the self-adjusting capabilities of the enterprise economy than exists today, and by the same token, less need for government intervention of any kind. In the second place, in so far as government intervention was called for, the prevailing orthodoxy tended to play up the virtues of monetary management as against fiscal policy. Indeed, when Secretary of the Treasury Mellon seized general prosperity by the forelock and made it the occasion for running a budgetary surplus and for paying back part of the government debt contracted during World War I, few there were to criticize the operation. Meanwhile there was great faith that the newly created Federal Reserve System would be more than capable of handling large swings in business activity. In his moving apologia to the Pecora investigating committee in 1933, the late Russell Leffingwell, a partner in J. P. Morgan and himself no mean student of economics, specifically mentioned the Federal Reserve as one reason among many to explain the exuberance and confidence of the 'twenties that prosperity could be indefinitely continued in what came to be known as a "New Era."

The crash of 1929 and subsequent events proved a rude shock to these expectations, and set the stage for the advent of new practices and ideas. As waspish critics never tire of pointing out, the Roosevelt administration was elected to office on a platform not only of protecting the integrity of the dollar but of fiscal retrenchment and a balanced budget. Within a year of arrival in office it had abandoned both pledges under circumstances that in retrospect, at least, appear highly paradoxical. In taking the country off the gold standard in the autumn of 1933 and through subsequent passage of the Gold Reserve Act of 1934, under which the dollar is no longer redeemable in gold at home, though gold is used to settle accounts abroad, the New Deal in fact greatly enlarged the powers of the Federal Reserve authorities to affect domestic credit and so stimulate enterprise. Yet even as this occurred, word went out that monetary policy was at best a weak reed toward this end. The Fed might greatly increase banks' reserves, but unless businessmen borrowed at the banks the operation was bound to be ineffective. As the saying goes, "you cannot push a string." Increasingly, the government chose to try to stimulate economic activity by other means—through relief payments, through public works, and through federal spending in general. With tax receipts still depressed, the budget continued out of balance. It was only a step from there to argue that such deficit spending, though small by present-day standards, was a kind of virtue, and to accept it as part of a new kind of orthodoxy.

This orthodoxy was in its turn greatly strengthened by the publication in 1936 of *The General Theory of Employment, Interest and Money* by John Maynard Keynes, whose views on wage matters we have referred to in the previous chapter. As noted, Keynes' ideas, properly understood, give scant encouragement to those who advocate wage increases in times of depression as a means of increasing purchasing power. At the same time Keynes drew a sharp distinction between what may be termed "voluntary" and "involuntary" unemployment. The first may occur if workers, through union pressure or otherwise, bid money wage rates up beyond marginal product, thus impinging on profits and profitable output. Involuntary unemployment occurs when there is a substantial drop in the price level, which in effect raises the level of *real* wages without workers having initiated the change. In these circumstances, Keynes argued, it is idle to try to cure the situation through general wage-cutting. Rather prices must be *reflated* upward by credit policy, and if that proves ineffective, by increased government spending. With some justice Keynes may be accused of playing a trick on the workers, because for his policy to work real wages must fall, though money wages remain stable. But within the trick there lies a worthwhile distinction. There is a profound difference between the situation where workers bargain themselves out of jobs by asking more than their services are worth and the situation where they are thrown out of jobs because most or all prices are falling as the result of general deflation.

If Keynes had stopped here he might have made a valid point, but scarcely would have introduced a

revolution in economic thought. He, of course, did
not stop with wage analysis. What gave his views
such tremendous influence was his attempt to show
that the enterprise economy could, so to speak, get
itself on dead center in a condition of mass unemployment, and stick there, unless jarred loose by massive government intervention. In developing this
thesis Keynes placed great emphasis on a way of looking at the economy which, though not original with
him, occupies a key place in his analytic. If we look at
the process of production, from its various sources to
its ultimate use, we can discern two main streams.
One is the flow of so-called "consumption goods"—
food, clothing, and even durables like automobiles—
which are bought by the ultimate consumer. The
other is the flow of so-called "capital goods"—machinery and tools of all kinds—which are bought by producers and which, when put to use, make the output
of consumption goods more efficient and less
onerous.

Such investment in capital goods generates income
for those employed in making them, no less than does
the output of consumer goods; and if all of this double flow of income were spent on consumption goods,
there would be an excess of demand for them and,
other things equal, a bidding up of prices. To make
the process work there must be abstention or saving
(Crusoe will have to get along with less fish during
the time he is making his nets to catch more fish in
the future), and this saving must pass smoothly over

into the investment process. If savings lag behind investment we shall, as the above implies, get inflation. But if, on the other hand, savings outstrip investment, we will get deflation and recession. For in this case people will be withholding income from the purchase of consumption goods without putting it to work in the making of capital goods. There will be a "leakage" in the intricate, over-all economic process which normally equates total supply and demand. And with this leakage production will fall back, with resources and workers unemployed.

Now, on traditional theory, such leakage is not apt to occur. For savings and investment are closely meshed together through the action of interest rates, which are determined by demand for capital, on the one hand, and the supply of savings, on the other. If this is true, then any slackening of investment, however occasioned, will tend to depress interest rates, and this will in turn tend to discourage savings and release income for consumption, while at the same time encouraging capital investment, thus reestablishing a new balance. Keynes challenged this assumption, partly on the grounds that in recession money will pile up in idle cash balances, and partly by arguing that consumption, saving, and investment are in the real world influenced by decisions that are uncoordinated with each other. As a result, attempts to save and attempts to invest can get seriously out of step, and as this happens income and output, and hence employment, will decline. The important point is that investment is the dynamic and volatile element of the economy, affecting both income and consumption, and a drop in investment may set off cumulative effects which put the whole machine out of order.

From this kind of analysis it might follow that government's efforts to stimulate and stabilize the economy in times of recession should be addressed primarily to restoring investment incentives and business confidence, and if this had been the aspect of Keynes' teaching seized on by economists and politicians, then the history of the depression years, and indeed, of our times, might well have been different. As matters turned out, this insight got lost in the shuffle of political events. What intrigued intellectuals of the 'thirties was that Keynes seemed to have shown that the modern economy is not self-propelling through the interaction of private forces, and that only increased government intervention on many fronts can save it from itself. At the end of *The General Theory,* while in one sense defending the virtues of the enterprise system, Keynes talks airily of a "somewhat comprehensive socialization of investment" in order to make capitalism work—a phrase pregnant with all kinds of political hazards. More obviously, in his popular writings as well as in his practical advice to government officials, he dramatized the idea that high levels of output in the economy depend not only on consumption and private investment but on government spending, which, especially if financed by deficits, may be regarded as complementary to private investment. It is the twin ideas that government outlays are, so to speak, on all fours with private outlays, and that deficit spending is a comprehensive cure for unemployment, that have given Keynes and his followers their unique impact.

4.

That impact has indeed been revolutionary in more ways than one, and yet, as we look back now on Keynesian assumptions and prescriptions, we must, I think, see large defects in both. In the first place, private investment, which seemed to him so anemic, has in fact proved to be far more robust than Keynes supposed, thanks to invention and the continuous progress of technology. In the second place, his bitter attack on the traditional virtues of thrift and saving seems wholly out of place in a world still racked by poverty and want over wide areas of the globe. While calling his work a "general" theory, Keynes in fact wrote a kind of *special* theory influenced at many points by the peculiar times in which he lived. Nor did he overthrow the great "classical" tradition of economics to which he himself owed so much. Rather, he added to it, providing us with fresh insights if we are wise enough to use them, but scarcely obsoleting the wisdom of the past. It is significant

OF MONEY AND SPENDING

111

that some modern economists of reputation who
have been strongly influenced by Keynes are now
calling themselves not neo-Keynesians, but *neo-clas-
sicists*. That is a step in the right direction and toward the correct kind of synthesis.

For the evidence multiplies that concentration on
the kind of "aggregate" economics of which Keynes
was so fond contains its own pitfalls; and the
evidence is even clearer that no single panacea, least
of all government spending, will achieve a healthy
and growing economy. This is, I suspect, the great
lesson of the depression 'thirties, when deficit spending was gingerly tried out, only to be negated by
other New Deal policies which served to undermine
business confidence and to kill off those "animal
spirits" on which Keynes himself set such great store.
But whatever may have been true for that gloomy
decade, it is apparent today that government spending cannot in itself be regarded as the solution for all
our ills, else they would have long since disappeared
under the impact of a federal budget that has now
risen to the $100 billion mark. As Professor Ray-
mond J. Saulnier, head of the Council of Economic
Advisers under President Eisenhower, has said:
"What recent history tells us about the effects of increases in federal spending is not very favorable to
the view that an economy such as ours can spend
itself into prosperity. . . . What this experience tells
us is that if the environment is not favorable to an

increase in private spending, an increase in federal spending, even a large increase, is a well nigh futile exercise."[2]

The point is well taken, and reinforces conclusions implicit in our whole analysis of employment and unemployment. In particular, we must realize that all efforts of the government to stimulate the economy will be self-defeating unless due emphasis is placed on wage behavior. For if money wages are constantly thrust up in bad times and in good, those responsible for credit and fiscal policies will find themselves on the horns of a dilemma. If they are passive they may well find that unemployment is spreading as the result of the squeeze on business profits. If they respond and "validate" the wage increases through easy money or spending, they risk putting the economy on the ratchet of inflation where wages and prices constantly edge up in competition with each other, to the great detriment of the consumer and of those seeking jobs. As the late Per Jacobsson, former head of the International Monetary Fund, emphasized: "In the past, countries which combined cost adjustments with credit expansion (in times of recession) have fared better than those that did not."[3] And in a dynamic economy it is essential that industries with high productivity gains be free to pass part of

[2] Raymond J. Saulnier, "The Growing Dialogue on Economic Growth."
[3] The Market Economy in the World of Today (Philadelphia: American Philosophical Society, 1961).

these gains out to the public in the form of lower prices rather than sluicing them into wage increases under the pressure of powerful unions.

This is one more reason, if added reason were needed, for bringing the unions under the discipline of laws that will reduce their extraordinary perquisites and privileges. Far from penalizing the worker, such reforms would make easier the cure of recessions and contribute to long-term growth. As that able economist and philosopher, David McCord Wright, has reminded us on more than one occasion, growth involves change, and change is at best uncomfortable for those involved in the process. As new industries and technologies arise, they will always displace some workers as well as some companies, and there is no help for that. What we can do is ease the transition by removing the restrictions which foreclose new job opportunities. Once more, if the climate and the environment are right, growth will occur spontaneously as the result of hundreds of thousands of individual decisions, which cannot be charted or predicted in advance. If the environment is not right, then much learned talk about growth and expansion by government officials and others becomes at best a kind of statistical parlor game and at worst a new invitation for Washington to try to direct and manipulate the entire economy.

Today the temptation to attempt such manipulation runs strong, not only because of misunderstanding concerning the multiple forces that make for growth, but also because of slavish addiction on the part of many economists to statistical comparisons and so-called "extrapolations," which, however useful to those who know their limitations, can be dangerous guides to policy. The usual argument is that if the economy's labor force is growing at, say, 1.5 per cent per year, and man-hour productivity is growing by, say, 2.5 per cent per year, then production *must* go up by at least 4 per cent per year if we are to maintain conditions of high employment. If this expansion does not occur, the experts declare that there is a production "gap" between actual and potential performance; and it is then argued that this gap must be filled by higher consumption, higher private investment, or more government spending, usually with strong emphasis on the latter curative.

We need not go here into all the learned dispute that goes on about this gap, especially when it is calculated over long time periods. I would emphasize that much that passes for wisdom in this matter comes down to what logicians call a tautology—a statement that is perfectly true but whose conclusion is inherent in the premises. The growth proposition says that if the labor force and productivity are going up, then output should advance. But it is just as true to say that if employment does not go up, and if unemployment stays large, then output will disap-

point us. Put this way, however, we should have to
address ourselves to all the causes of such unemployment before we would be sure of the proper cure,
and thus we are right back to all of the multiple
problems with which so many able economists in our
day and in the past have wrestled—the problem of
the business cycle, of business incentives, and of costs
and prices, to mention but a few. To wish these away
by the new mechanistic analysis of growth and
growthmanship is really to adjourn all serious economic discussion.

5.

We cannot, I think, afford this luxury, and in conclusion let us try to draw the strings of the argument
together and to put both monetary and fiscal policy
in their proper perspective. The all-important proposition is that growth and expansion do in the end
depend on private forces, and that the proper role of
government is to set the framework for releasing
them. In doing so government has a constitutional
obligation to provide the economy with a reliable
money system in which the value of the dollar is not
constantly eroded away. Here good men may differ.
As we shall see in a later chapter, some economists
believe we can only solve the money problem by return to gold coinage and the gold standard. Other
eminent economists, notably Professor Milton Fried-

man of the University of Chicago, argue that we are stuck with an irredeemable paper system, but that this system can be greatly improved.[4] Specifically, they hold that we can best achieve both price stability and growth by adopting a *fixed rule* for the gradual increase of the money supply, rather than depending on the discretion of the federal reserve authorities to outguess every twist and turn of the business cycle.

Such long-term proposals deserve debate and consideration but should not blind us to present realities. As a practical matter, and under the monetary system as it stands, the Federal Reserve is our first line of defense against both inflation and deflation, and needs all the protection we can give it against undue political influence. In so far as the Reserve authorities must choose between trying to overcome unemployment and their basic franchise to maintain a sound and dependable currency, they should give clear priority to the latter objective. For over the years the protection of the integrity of the dollar, both at home and abroad, should in itself contribute to high levels of output and to real, rather than spurious, economic growth. It takes courage to act on that assumption today, but it is a safer assumption than the cynical view that a "little inflation" really does not matter. For it is in periods of monetary inflation that recessions are bred.

It is also time to rethink and redefine the true aims

[4] *A Program for Monetary Stability* (New York: Fordham University Press, 1959).

of fiscal policy. As compared to monetary measures it is an exceedingly clumsy instrument. It takes relatively little time for the Reserve authorities to change their stance as regards tightening or loosening credit. It takes months for the government to increase spending or for Congress to enact a new tax bill. Indeed, by the time the spenders have gotten their projects in order, the recession they are trying to fight may well be past, and spending, once started, is extremely difficult to stop. Thus it comes about that a policy of countercyclical spending usually results in an ever-enlarging budget. The deficits come along, often at the wrong time, but the surpluses somehow rarely appear. This should not be understood to mean that the budget should be in perfect balance at all times. If in a period of declining business activity revenues fall short of expectations, it would be foolish to raise taxes. Rather, the resulting deficit should be allowed to have its effect. But such temporary deficits caused by a fall-off in the tax receipts are very different from planned deficits to meet the alleged need of the economy for growth. There is something to the idea that the budget can be a built-in stabilizer. But a stabilizer should stabilize and not be constantly torn apart.

Finally, it should be remarked that a stabilizer does not have to be of overwhelming size to be effective, and there is no logical connection between a budgetary policy aimed at stabilizing the economy and an ever-growing volume of government expenditures. Acceptance of such connection is one of the more dangerous illusions of those economists who are today enmeshed and entranced by the "gap" theory of real and potential output. It is inherent in much that has passed for wisdom in discussion of economic policy. But it is illusion all the same. If the U.S. budget were held around present levels or reduced, we should still get the benefits of compensatory fiscal action, since in recession tax receipts would fall, while in boom they would rise. If there is advantage in this kind of compensation, the advantage can be obtained without incessant growth of government functions. The important point is that *one does not have to be in favor of absolute budget balance in every year in order to be against growth in government expenditures every year.*

The distinction, while obvious, is nevertheless of enormous importance in the larger task of maintaining limited government and the market economy. Accepting it, we can grant that fiscal as well as monetary policy has a place in maintaining the free system without succumbing to the blandishments of big-government advocates. How much the government should spend on defense and other functions can be fought out *on the merits* without becoming involved in spurious arguments about maintaining economic prosperity. Meanwhile we should press on with overhauling our crazy-quilt tax structure, not with the objective of creating new deficits, which seems to be the purpose of all too many government officials, but rather with the objective of releasing personal and corporate *incentives* on which growth, progress, and federal revenues depend. But tax reform depends on keeping expenditures under control if its promise is not to be frittered away in further inflation. The job of accomplishing this will not be easy, given the present drift of political opportunism. But at least such opportunism should no longer have the support of perverted economic doctrine.

CHAPTER VII

Of the "starved" public sector

"The more it snows
　　(Tiddely pom)
The more it goes
　　(Tiddely pom)
The more it goes
　　(Tiddely pom)
On snowing."
—A. A. MILNE, *The House at Pooh Corner*

WE MUST NOW DESCEND from the rarified atmosphere of monetary and fiscal theory to the stuffier confines of the budget bureau and the Bureau of Internal Revenue. For this pedestrian journey we shall need a guide, and Washington has long provided one. The proffered aid takes the form of a so-called "pie chart," which indicates that of every dollar the government spends the largest portion by far goes to national defense, social security, interest payments on past debt, and other "intractable" items, so that the margin for economy and economizing is practically non-existent. Armed with this device, among others, and buttressed too by the fact that these days the federal government keeps, not one set of books, but no less than three, any director of the budget worth his salt can demonstrate that even if big government spending weren't good for the country, it is all but impossible to stem the tide.

Let us admit at the outset that it has been quite a tide. The over-all figures are, of course, familiar, and yet they bear repeating at a time when it is said that the "public sector" of the American economy, or, to be blunt about it, *the government sector*, is really in a pretty starved condition—considering, at least, the needs of the nation as defined by something still more intangible, the "national purpose." In his immensely popular book, *The Affluent Society*,[1] John Kenneth Galbraith goes out of his way to dramatize the paucity of our public facilities as compared to the luxury and waste of private economic activity. This thesis is manna to not a few politicians who in less sophisticated times might have been brushed aside as "pork-barrel" specialists. It has subtly inspired many a presidential message on the state of the nation and the state of the budget. It has even been treated with respect by a commentator of the stature of Walter Lippmann, who, as far back as the presidential election of 1960, opined that "The Republican Party under Eisenhower does not understand

1 (Boston: Houghton Mifflin Company, 1958).

the necessity of greater allocation of our resources, in a growing economy, to public needs."

Unhappily, however, Mr. Eisenhower, like other Presidents both before and after him, seems to have understood this alleged "necessity" all too well. Consider the record, as told by the raw figures. In the distant years of the late 'twenties, expenditures of the federal government ran to about $2.8 billion. By 1940 the New Deal, in its role, as Mr. Roosevelt phrased it, of Dr. Beat-the-Depression, had pushed the figure up to $9.1 billion. When this doctor was dismissed and Dr. Win-the-War took over, expenditures soared up of necessity to nearly $100 billion, declining thereafter and rising again to $74 billion in 1953 under the impact of the Korean War. Then a strange thing happened, apparently unnoticed by Mr. Lippmann. Committed to economy, the Eisenhower administration did reduce military outlays somewhat in its first term in office. But in Mr. Eisenhower's second term, prefaced by a budget message wherein he stated that the people "demand and . . . deserve" certain services, *non-military* outlays rose by 33 per cent, bringing total expenditures in fiscal 1961 to $81.5 billion. From there President Kennedy carried the ball, increasing both military and non-military outlays with impartiality and driving total outlays close to the $100 billion mark. From that politically unpalatable figure President Johnson drew back with an initial 1965 budget of "economy and progress," which held the line at $97.9 billion.

But, in fact, federal spending has broken through the $100 billion barrier when we count the huge operations of social security and other trust funds (old age insurance, railroad retirement, etc.). Adding these to the regular budget, we find that total cash outlays, euphemistically called "payments to the public," ran in 1964 to $122.7 billion. Meanwhile, of course, the states and local communities have also been doing *their* duty, with expenditures rising from $8.4 billion in 1940 to an estimated $69.5 billion in 1964. Piling this on top of federal cash outlays we get a grand total of some $190 billion, which must be paid for in one way or another—by taxes, borrowing, or inflation. This, indeed, reflects affluence of a kind, but it is somewhat different from the kind of affluence suggested by the title of Professor Galbraith's famous book. It is the affluence of a government structure which, as the saying goes, has never had it quite so good.

It will be pointed out, of course, that while the burden of government has certainly grown, so have the shoulders of the economy. Whereas it is estimated that in 1940 total government outlays, federal, state, and local, ran to 18.4 per cent of the national product, today they run *only* to about 30 per cent—a rise, to be sure, but a smaller one than the raw figures indicate. This is an important point but not necessarily a decisive one. The English economist Colin Clark has argued—and it was an argument that impressed Keynes —that when governments take more than 25 per cent of the national product the results will be inflationary, even if the whole amount is covered by taxes. Moreover, as we shall see, taxes have been exerting a tremendous drag on the economy, undermining incentives and producing all kinds of distorting side effects. The power to tax and to spend is the power to destroy, and if government were one day to pre-empt 50 per cent of the economy, we should have subtly collectivized the country without the advocates of socialism and statism having fired a shot.

2.

Thus there is good reason to restrain expenditures and to work toward a more rational and less burdensome tax system. The place to dig in is at the federal level, where concentration of power is most dangerous in a federal republic. Unhappily, it is precisely here that the men with the pie charts have an initial advantage by being able to point out that over half of all federal budgetary outlays are for the defense of the country—an undisputed function of the central government. When one considers what the U.S. and its allies owe to our military power, one will not be inclined to stint the needs of the Pentagon. Moreover defense is highly technical, and few laymen feel competent to judge it. What the laymen can emphasize is that defense spending of the present magnitude does constitute a difficult lump for any free economy to digest, even though most of the

great contracting firms are privately owned and re
sponsive to market forces. Dependence on a single
monopoly buyer exacts a hidden cost of the competitive system which does not show up in the raw statistics. And on more than one occasion the government
has exerted its power to determine issues that have
nothing to do with preserving the safety of the
country. Witness the manner in which the Kennedy
administration threatened to switch defense orders
away from steel firms that, rightly or wrongly, sought
to raise prices in 1962.

On the face of it, therefore, the efforts of the Johnson administration to trim defense spending came as
welcome news, though the manner in which the cuts
are being made is more debatable. Thus far the axe
has fallen chiefly on military procurement and on
outlays for research and development which have
maintained the U.S. lead in advanced weaponry.
Meanwhile spending for the upkeep of conventional
forces goes on at record levels. The U.S. undoubtedly
needs army and navy forces ready for situations like
that in Lebanon in 1958, when troops had to be
landed to restore order. But it is by no means clear
that the country needs as many as sixteen army divisions and three Marine divisions for fighting so-
called brush fire wars. As General Eisenhower,
among others, perceived, this kind of readiness is
exceedingly costly in a day when it takes some $10,000
per year to support each man in uniform, quite aside

from putting weapons and other equipment into his hands. In the opinion of a good many experts, the maintenance of huge conventional forces dissipates money better spent in maintaining U.S. long-range technological superiority.

In addition there is need for making minor cuts in the defense budget of the kind urged by the Hoover Commission as far back as 1949, and by a recent report of the Chamber of Commerce, which pointed out that the armed services are engaged in some two thousand commercial and industrial activities, many of which should be turned back to private hands. There is also need for reconsidering at least two large programs which are often viewed as collateral to the national defense effort—space exploration and foreign aid. The former, now costing $5 billion, can presumably yield national advantages if defense as well as exploration is kept in mind in the projects underwritten. But the popular arguments for just "shooting the moon" as a way of preserving the national "image" have lost some of their appeal now that the Russians have been invited to go along in the enterprise. With respect to foreign aid, it is one thing to bolster by indirect means such outposts as Formosa and Korea. It is quite another thing to justify all foreign aid as a defense of the "free world" against communism—the more so because not a few countries receiving it are either avowed "neutrals" or, as in the case of Yugoslavia, already far inside the communist camp.

3.

But it is in the realm of domestic spending, which has nothing to do with defense, space, or even foreign aid, that recent budgets have been most vulnerable. Precisely because military expenditures are so high, it would be only prudent to cut down elsewhere. The really discouraging thing is that, whether Republicans or Democrats are in office, non-defense spending continues to climb. Whereas in 1954 this spending constituted less than 30 per cent of the regular budget, it rose in the mid-'sixties to nearly 40 per cent, and to much more than that if we count in social security payments. It is this trend which needs to be checked, if not reversed, and in doing so we need to emphasize two basic principles.

The first is that in a federal system the central government should not undertake duties that can be as well cared for by the individual states. Dollars are shrunk rather than enlarged by being transferred to Washington and then back again to local communities. The second principle involves drawing a basic distinction between the words "public" and "governmental." Advocates of an enlarged "public sector" have subtly confused discourse by implying that if there is a public need, then government must fill it. But this is surely not the case. In the American, and indeed in most Western communities, private industry meets the overwhelming body of "public" needs, if these are defined as the provision of food, clothing, and shelter, no less than luxuries. Moreover, there are all kinds of public services involving education, health, and welfare which are best accomplished by private associations which are neither governmental nor strictly commercial. This free collaborative activity, plus the contribution of enterprise itself, could be far larger than it is today if the federal government in particular would reduce its own sprawling activity, which all too often simply jams the system.

The most conspicuous case in point is agriculture, where, as we have seen, government price supports are causing great damage to the market economy without benefiting those whom they are supposed to serve—the small and indigent farmer. A responsible policy of lowering supports and eliminating controls would both benefit the farm community and eventually save the taxpayer $3 to $4 billion per year, to say nothing of reducing our wasteful surpluses, which now run to over $7 billion. Other economies, though less dramatic, press for attention. There is a case, for instance, for the "development of national resources" (now costing some $2.6 billion per year) if this only meant true conservation of forest land and natural wonders, so close to the heart of Theodore Roosevelt. Nor must we question the need for dredging the Mississippi and other waterways in the interest of transportation and flood control. But the feckless manner in which river development has been turned into a drive to

substitute government-generated electric power for
private power is something else again.

It is an uncomfortable fact that the Tennessee
Valley Authority, originally justified to develop
hydroelectric power, now increasingly uses coal and
steam facilities which could just as well be put up by
private industry. The government is also spending
many millions on new electric facilities which will
join the power grids of the Pacific Northwest and the
Southwest, justifying the project on grounds of profitability. But if it is profitable, then the whole rationale
for government action collapses, unless socialization
of private power is our aim. "Socialization" is, of
course, a dirty word not found in the lexicon of ardent
government activists. What is found is an expensive
habit of pushing the nose of the federal camel into the
enterprise tent, plus a curiously dated faith in the
philosophy of overhead planning.

The Department of the Interior teems with projects which would not only survey and resurvey the
nation's natural resources, but would lay down guidelines as to how coal, minerals, water power, and the
oceans themselves are to be utilized this year and fifty
years from now. The harm in such exercises is not in
the estimates made. The harm lies in the implicit
assumption that government will guide the whole
process irrespective, usually, of technological developments which, on the record, can obsolete the most
meticulous of blueprints overnight. The U.S. has not
yet adopted a five-year plan, as popularized by Russia,

India, France, and a score of lesser nations. But if such a plan is born, it is a safe bet that, in the language of the track, it will be *out* of Interior *by* that old French warhorse, *Dirigisme*.

Many other areas of the budget call for pruning, but those who would use the shears must be expert in prying beneath the figures. Expenditures for commerce and transportation, for instance, run to over $3 billion in the President's administrative budget; but they are more than double that if one adds in highway trust fund outlays. Expenditures for housing and community development still seem relatively small, but the figures that show are only the tip of the iceberg. It is estimated that at present the total federal involvement in housing through guaranties and subsidies runs to over $100 billion—or a third as large as the recorded national debt. A big part of this involvement results from the operations of the Federal Housing Administration, which, set up as a depression measure, deserves credit for setting a new pattern in home finance which private lenders have followed. It is harder to see, however, why FHA still has to insure some 15 per cent of all non-farm housing starts, why its responsibilities should be constantly expanded into other fields, and why we need in addition the parallel activities of the Veterans Administration, plus the multi-billion-dollar operations of the Federal National Mortgage Association (Fannie May), which buys up mortgages whenever it thinks the market is depressed.

Moreover, it should be noted that, having set in motion a great era of private home building, mostly in the suburbs, government administrators are now far from content with the extent of their handiwork. They are giving increased attention to what, to borrow a phrase from the late Lincoln Steffens, may be called "the shame of the cities." Urban development and the elimination of crime-breeding city slums are now the main targets, and such development involves far more than self-liquidating mortgage insurance. Forward commitments for urban renewal grants now run to over $3 billion, and, despite bitter criticism, payments for public housing, where government in effect actually owns the new facilities, have mounted in the past four years. President Johnson has repeated President Kennedy's plea for a Cabinet-level Department of Housing and Community Development, and the trend toward ever larger government involvement in this field continues.

Yet it may be doubted whether more federal spending from the top down is really the way to solve America's housing problem, such as it is. The fundamental impediments to improving the American city in particular lie in distorted tax laws which penalize improvements on existing buildings (which, after all, house the great majority of the population); in slum-breeding rent control legislation which is still on the books in New York; and in the high costs exacted by building codes and the building trade unions—to mention but a few. Many of these impediments have been built in at the state and local level, and more federal spending simply serves to divert attention from needed corrections. When all is said and done, government cannot possibly re-house America; this is the business of private industry. What governments at all levels can do is establish the framework and the rules within which private and semi-private effort can take hold. But this involves painstaking and, on the whole, undramatic reform with low vote-getting potential. It is easier, though infinitely less effective, to multiply "programs" and "plans" which will be paid for tomorrow than to face up to the realities that must be coped with today.

4.

While housing still waits for its ultimate federal coordinator, we already have a Cabinet-level Department of Health, Education, and Welfare, and the results of creating it have been, as might have been expected, a great proliferation of federal activities. Expenditures in this area—plus outlays for "labor" (manpower retraining, etc.)—run to over $7 billion per year, with the operations of the multi-billion Social Security trust funds piled on top of that. The rationale of this enormous involvement is the "strengthening of human resources," which is, of course, in the language of the times, an all-important "national purpose." Agreed. But this does not mean that reaching it necessarily depends on government.

In the field of health it is worth reminding ourselves that the American public spends over $20 billion for private medical care, that nearly 80 per cent of the civilian population now has some form of health insurance, and that this figure is growing because of individual and corporate effort. It is hard to see why the National Institutes of Health should finance an estimated two-thirds of all health research, wasting taxpayer money on investigations of "information contained in echoes" and on "the ontogeny of English phrase structure." "As the research effort has grown," states a recent budget message, "the need for additional competent researchers has become more urgent," and so more must be spent for training "research specialists." But if and as the specialists become available, there will have, of course, to be more projects of one kind or another to absorb them. The government complains that the number of doctors in the country is falling behind population growth, and makes this a further argument for aid. But in other fields it would be dangerous to correlate need with population increase, forgetting the factor of efficiency and technological advance. Nor does it seem to occur to Washington that the number of doctors in a country depends in the last analysis on the attractions of the profession. In Britain the shortage of trained medical personnel has gone hand in hand with the progressive socialization of medicine.

Pressure for increased federal aid to education is based on the same kind of faulty reasoning, about the shortage of both facilities and teachers. This is the theme of most recent budget messages and lies behind the drive to make a "deeper commitment" to all forms of education, including aid to the country's public school system. Propaganda for such a deeper commitment overlooks the fact that, by and large, Americans have generously supported their educational institutions, both public and private. Whereas since the turn of the century public school enrollment has more than doubled, expenditures for the schools by states and local communities have gone up over eightyfold—from $215 million in 1899–1900 to more than $18 billion in the 'sixties. As a result of this expansion, the classroom shortage in the U.S. public schools has been rapidly diminishing, and has in some communities turned into a surplus. Meanwhile, teachers' salaries have been rising proportionately faster in recent years than the U.S. per capita income or industrial wages, and the number of workers in the labor force. The fundamental need of the future is not just for more money for schools, but for more and better schooling for the money. This is an objective best achieved by keeping control of the public schools at the local community level, where their day-to-day problems are known and can be thrashed out. Intervention by the federal government cannot solve these problems, while it does raise the danger that Washington will some day try, not just to finance education, but to control it.

This danger is already apparent in the financial assistance—direct and indirect—which the federal government is now giving to higher education. Through the National Defense Education Act of 1958, Washington provides loans and fellowships to college students and makes substantial loans for college dormitories. The National Science Foundation contributes to so-called "basic research," defined as almost any kind of scientific inquiry. Such research is also financed through the National Aeronautics and Space Administration, so that the total federal money going to the colleges and universities for research of one kind or another is estimated at $1.5 billion per year. Sharp controversy about the loyalty oath and how Harvard University should use a government-financed cyclotron suggest that federal aid does bring federal influence and control. Nor will fears on this score be allayed by the suggestion that the government should be just as much interested in the teaching of the "social sciences" as it is in the teaching of the natural sciences—a statement which, if implemented, might well give increased weight, if not prestige, to the "new economics" of government spending. It would be neither foolish nor premature to believe that much government assistance to education is currently oriented in the wrong direction.

The strength of the American educational system lies in its multiplicity of means and in its diffusion of power and authority. Even in the case of primary education, the country might be better off if state and local governments, while insisting on minimal educational standards, yielded their now near-monopoly on school facilities, giving tax relief to those who choose to send their children to private schools. But while such a plan is still utopian, it is not utopian to believe that the federal government certainly should curtail rather than expand its growing power and influence at all levels of the educational process. Dollars taxed for Harvard mean fewer dollars available for private donations or for state and local use. But the argument goes beyond that. As Friedrich Hayek has said: "Nowhere is freedom more important than where our ignorance is greatest—at the boundaries of knowledge." The lasting contribution which government can make to education is to keep that freedom secure and those boundaries open.

We come, finally, to the role of government in caring for those who, whether educated or not, have lost their footing in a society which we would like to think increasingly provides opportunity for all. It was the confident hope of government officials that when the U.S. adopted the Social Security Act of 1935, providing for old age and disability insurance and giving powerful impetus to state unemployment insurance, there would be a diminution over the years of other forms of aid to the destitute, and for relief purposes. That hope has only partly been fulfilled. Federal relief, which ran high in the 'thirties, tapered off in the war years, but since then has steadily edged upward. In fiscal 1964, grants to the states for subsidiary old age assistance, aid to dependent children, aid to the blind, and for other purposes ran to some $3 billion, or over half the total relief burden. The justification for this rising commitment toward centralization is that poorer states lack the taxing potential to take care of their own. One may question this thesis. Granted that much destitution exists among the "underemployed" of the southern states, it is still true that indigent men and women may be worse off in the great cities of the richer industrial areas than on the land. Once more, dollars do not grow bigger by being taxed away to Washington to be processed and doled out again, at the risk of great political corruption. Relief of destitution should be fundamentally a responsibility of the states and local communities, where it can be integrated with the not inconsiderable and not-to-be despised work of private charity of all kinds.

This is doubly true because Washington has preempted, probably permanently, the job of trying to "insure" all citizens against the hazards of old age and disability through basic social security legislation. Total payments of the old age trust fund now run to well over $16 billion per year, and will grow as population expands. The system is now so deeply embedded in the economy that it must be regarded as a permanent fixture in American life. But this surely does not mean that it should be indefinitely expanded. It must be recognized that old age benefits, as currently administered, are not in fact based on the insurance principle, but are to a large degree

transfers of money from the present working population to those in retirement. Moreover, the system
suffers from both its coercive character and the fact
that its whole machinery is concentrated in government hands. No effort has been made to give citizens
a choice between using this federal machinery or
alternative private institutions. No recognition is
given the man who prudently, by his own efforts,
takes steps to care for himself and his family.

In view of all this, the continued effort to expand
the Social Security system to cover medical care for
the aged is wholly suspect. In the last analysis, the
"Medicare" proposal is a new form of class legislation—another effort to appeal to and to build up a
political pressure group, of which we have surely had
enough. The U.S. is rich enough to afford help to its
needy. It has, let us grant, a long journey to make in
the elimination of poverty and distress. But the diminution of poverty is a long-term job, depending on
larger output of goods and services, the elimination
of barriers now preventing those able and willing
to work from finding jobs, and the eradication of
specific pockets of distress which, as anyone who has
troubled to visit eastern Kentucky or West Virginia
knows, are real enough. In this task government
agencies can help, but only as they are viewed as
supplementary to private effort. Welfare in the end
is everybody's business—the business of the corporation, the union, the church, the individual. Fiscal
prudence, no less than common sense, should make

us sharply distinguish between the "public good" and increasing the already vast sphere of central government spending, and its concomitant, the burden of taxation.

5.

For taxes are, of course, the other side of the spending coin, and their cumulative impact has increased in direct proportion to outlays. This impact has been somewhat concealed by the withholding tax device, which is a boon to the Treasury and a kind of tranquilizer for the population. Withholding taxes for all kinds of social security alone now run to several times the *total* of all federal taxes paid at the beginning of World War II—a pointed reminder that welfare is not a free gift of a beneficent state, which in the last analysis has nothing to "give." The nation's tax load federal, state, and local now runs to about $160 billion; this works out to about $2,800 per household or $840 per capita. As the budget has grown to a document of some 1,600 pages, so too has the Internal Revenue Code, which runs to more than 1,000 pages in its own right, with thousands of pages of opinions added to that; and in this case the print is very fine indeed. The proliferation of taxes has no doubt "created" jobs for an army of lawyers and accountants in all parts of the land. But the all-too-lively hand of the tax collector in the pockets of individuals and business enterprise alike has undoubtedly also served to take jobs away from men and women who need them more than the well-paid experts of Washington and Wall Street.

The critical first step in lightening the tax burden is undoubtedly to bring expenditures under control; this would give us a breathing period in which to reshape a crazy tax structure that has, in recent years, rarely balanced the budget but has, on the evidence, stifled and perverted the *incentives* which are necessary to a growth economy. The objective of tax reduction and reform, let us repeat, is not to give the economy a fortuitous and temporary "shot in the arm"; we have heard more than enough from those who think they know precisely how to manipulate the tax break and the spending accelerator in a way which will eliminate every zig and zag of the business cycle. The objective of tax reform—meaning the *reshaping of tax rates rather than the plugging of loopholes*—is to increase the basic motivations of the private economy on which in the end both jobs and revenue depend.

The case for such a reform is apparent in both the personal income tax, which now collects about 50 per cent of all administrative budget receipts, and, perhaps even more, in the corporation profit tax. Adopted in 1913, the personal income tax seemed a fairly innocuous measure, with a basic rate of only 1 per cent on the lowest bracket of taxable income and a top rate of 7 per cent. Then came the depression, and under bipartisan "leadership" the rate structure was wrenched upward to a range of 4 per

cent at the bottom and a destructive 63 per cent at
the top. World War II saw further rate increases and
lowering of exemptions which bore down not only
on the rich but also on the midle classes, while inflation increased the burden even while seeming to
lighten it. In the post-war years, the harried house-
holder running fast simply to stay in the same place
became a familiar sight. In 1962, a married couple
with two children who had a gross income of $7,500
in 1942 would have had to have an income of over
$14,000 in order to be as well off after taxes and
inflation as it had been twenty years earlier. Fortunately, people continue to move up the income
ladder, to the great benefit of themselves and society.
But at some point a progressive rate structure of 20
to 91 per cent was bound to weaken incentive, distort judgments, and to make the tax scoop an instrumentality for flattening out every economic recovery
without necessarily covering mounting Treasury
outlays.

The tax reduction program set in train by the
Kennedy administration and passed by the Johnson
administration may be a tentative first step, but only
that, toward correcting matters. In revising rates
downward to a low of 14 per cent at the bottom and
70 per cent at the top, it affords relief to those with
very large incomes, to the benefit, it is to be hoped,
of investment and the flow of risk capital. At the
same time, the initial effect of lowering the base rate
is to take some million and a half people off the tax

rolls entirely, thus temporarily diminishing revenues and increasing inflationary dangers. The larger criticism of the program is that it still leaves us with a highly progressive rate structure, whose gradient over the years needs to be further flattened.

How far we should go in this direction involves partly choice of philosophy, partly more practical considerations. It has long been the contention of many eminent economists that the whole principle of progression is morally wrong, since it involves in theory and in practice a redistribution of income from rich to poor which is no business of the modern state, and that once progression is adopted there is no clear-cut *rule* to define the scope of taxation. The ideal from this point of view is a return to the rule of "proportionality," wherein the rich pay more than the poor, but all pay on the same standard. Over a century ago, the economist McCulloch argued that once this standard was abandoned, we should be left "without rudder or compass" in a sea of troubles. Considering how things have gone, it will not do to laugh off this dictum.

One need not go this far, however, to believe that the egalitarian argument for sharp progression is thoroughly suspect, and that the path of sanity lies in a continued reversal of the trends of the past thirty years. Given economic expansion and rising incomes, there should be increasing room to maneuver in readjusting rates while still meeting basic revenue needs. Some see an ideal rate structure ranging from

14 per cent to 25 per cent in the not-too-distant future. More immediately, we would be accomplishing a lot if the top limit of the personal income tax were reduced from 70 to 50 per cent—a step that is thoroughly practical when one considers that *all rates above 50 per cent have in recent years brought in less than 2 per cent* of Treasury receipts. This single statistic sheds a vast amount of light on a maze of conflicting claims and counterclaims. The fact is that the tax burden cannot be indefinitely shifted upward. It can occasionally be eased to allow the people enduring it to walk a little more upright—and a little faster.

6.

To that end, we should also press on with the further reduction of the corporation profit tax, not in the interests of "buttering up" businessmen but of creating more real output, hence income, in the economy. Once again, the recent reduction of this tax from an over-all 52 per cent to 48 per cent represents a beginning—but only a beginning, and a meager one at that. Unlike high-bracket personal income taxes, the corporate levy does cream off much revenue —some $20 billion per year—but it does so fraudulently, and in a way which dries up other sources of potential receipts. There exists ample evidence that a large part of the corporation profits tax can be and is *passed on* to the public in the form of higher prices or lower wages than would otherwise obtain. To the degree that this actually occurs, the corporation tax is a kind of concealed sales or payroll tax, whose chief virtue is its deceptiveness, hence its ease of collection. The argument that the tax is good because it restrains the "monopoly profits" of capitalism breaks down on the evidence that the man in the street, not the capitalist, pays most of it.

Nor is this the sole reason for viewing the corporation profit tax as an imposter in an enterprise system. For whether all of the tax can be passed on or not, businessmen must seek to lessen its impact, and so they behave very differently than if it were not present. While this is true of most taxes, the profits tax is unique because, as emphasized in a recent study of the Tax Foundation, "business is society's chief agency for organizing capital and labor to produce, and to produce more rather than less efficiently." The personal income tax may dull incentives, but the corporation tax does more, striking directly at the nerve center of far-reaching decisions about prices, wages, employment, depreciation, and investment. In distorting those decisions it inevitably penalizes the public at large.

The distortions are of course manifold and well recognized. The furor over the misuse of corporate expense accounts is a small but revealing phenomenon. Since under the tax as it has stood for some years most corporately earned dollars are worth only forty-eight cents, there is an inevitable tendency for employees to load expenses on the employer and for the employer to be more lax in accepting them than he otherwise would be. In similar fashion, the tax tends to encourage corporations to go into debt, since interest can be charged off before the tax is paid —an escape often open to big, established firms but not to new ventures. Equally important, the tax encourages corporations to finance new investment through depreciation as well as retained earnings, rather than go out into the capital markets to raise new equity. There are those who seem to think that this is a good thing—notably Mr. Adolf Berle, who has argued that this practice gives our economic system greater stability. But it should also be noted that Mr. Berle uses the phenomenon of internal corporate financing to prove that the free competitive market is on the decline in the United States, and, as noted earlier, Berle seems to favor the kind of corporate statism where big business, big labor, and big government call the turn. For those of us who do not look on this denouement with favor, one of the principal arguments against the corporation tax is its discrimination against new risk ventures in favor of the big and established enterprise.

Beyond all these distortions, the fact remains that the corporation tax acts as a general brake on new investment, since in effect it doubles the amount which the corporation must earn or try to earn to justify such outlays. This inhibiting effect has been recognized in congressional efforts to stimulate investment by liberalized depreciation schedules and a tax credit for capital spending. The latter provision, however, is in itself highly discriminatory. True "reform" should look, not to more tax gimmicks, but to the progressive reduction to not more than 25 per cent, if not to the complete elimination, of the corporation tax. Reduction would have to be accompanied by concomitant cuts in high-bracket personal income taxes, and possibly some change in the treatment of capital gains, for otherwise corporations would be under even sharper pressure than they are today to withhold dividends and to pile up liquidity. But, as already seen, there is an overwhelming case, standing on its own merits, for taking the progression out of the personal income tax, so that corporate tax reform and personal income tax reform can go hand in hand. The probable results of combining the reforms would be to increase the flow of money into capital markets, to channel investment into more efficient use, and to release incentives all around.

And what of the anxious experts in the Treasury Department and the Bureau of the Budget? As already noted, sharp reduction in the progression of the personal income tax would not lose much revenue, for the top rates bring in very little now. Reduction in the corporation tax would initially lose revenue, for it is admittedly a powerful scoop. Yet here we must again remind ourselves of a point repeatedly made when considering federal spending.

Tax dollars are not enlarged by passing from the public to Washington and back again to the states. In somewhat similar fashion, the total federal tax take is not enlarged by sucking out of the corporation money which will in turn be extracted from the public through higher prices or lower wages if the tax is passed on, or, in any case, result in lower investment. Always provided that competition does its work, a reduction in the corporation tax should result in larger dividends to the public in higher wages to labor, in increased productivity as capital is economically invested, and in lower prices to consumers. This lays the basis for larger revenues through non-corporate forms of taxation and for steadier and faster economic growth, on which all tax revenues —federal, state, and local—in the long run depend.

Thus in the end true tax reform, coupled with control of the budget, offer an exciting alternative to the present dreary prospect of continued deficit finance and enlargement of the federal government's power. Whether one stresses tax reform first and curtailment of federal spending later or reverses the emphasis is to some degree a matter of political tactics. We need not indulge in futile debate about the "Puritan ethic" to resolve these claims and counterclaims. Prudence no less than vision dictates the dual course of reforming the tax structure while at the same time restricting the federal government to the tasks that it alone can accomplish, reserving

the rest "to the states respectively, or to the people."
The results of doing this would not be to jeopardize
the vital defense of U.S. interests abroad or its needs
at home. It would be to enhance a more puissant, productive, and free America.

CHAPTER VIII

Of
Gold and the international order

"A merchant of great traffic through the world."
—Shakespeare

WHILE THE CASE for sound money and for fiscal prudence, outlined in the last two chapters, has been made chiefly on domestic grounds, it is greatly strengthened when one comes to consider U.S. economic relations with the outside world. For while it may be convenient to look at many aspects of the economy as if the U.S. were a "closed" system, self-sufficient unto itself, this—as the British say—"is not the position." The economic development of the U.S. has been and is vitally dependent on world trade, whether we look at matters from the point of view of the exporter, or of industries importing foreign iron ore, copper, and a long list of other materials and end products. Total U.S. private investment abroad now runs to over $65 billion, and peripatetic trips to Europe and the Far East are not exactly confined to *Vogue*'s "jet set." Indeed, it is commonplace to remark that the horizons of U.S. business are now world-wide and that the U.S. bears a unique responsibility for developing a sound international economic order, in which both trade and investment can expand still further.

This depends to no little degree on knocking down trade barriers and in fostering a more hospitable climate abroad for private enterprise—tasks that will presently concern us. Yet it is safe to say that the prime condition for healthy world commerce is an acceptable *payments system* between nations, and free convertibility of one national currency into another. It was the great virtue of the gold standard, as developed by Britain in the nineteenth century and to which the U.S. adhered from shortly after the Civil War to the 1930's, that it made such convertibility easy and indeed highly automatic. Under the gold standard in its heyday, nations contracted to make their currencies fully convertible in gold, not only abroad but usually at home, and it followed that relatively small movements of gold from country to country had important domestic consequences. In the familiar textbook case, a nation whose imports exceeded its exports found itself losing gold. This loss forced it to tighten up on credit at home, thus depressing prices and incomes, which in turn helped to restrain imports and to stimulate exports. Nations acquiring gold were expected to react in opposite fashion, and through this elaborate signalling system national price levels tended to move "in step" with each other, and payments difficulties tended to be temporary. Thus the gold standard, while requiring skillful management, imposed a discipline both on external and internal events—a discipline which on the record contributed mightily to world economic development.

Today we live under what is sometimes called the "gold exchange standard," in which the discipline of gold has been relaxed but by no means altogether eliminated. As noted in Chapter VI, the U.S. gold stock still serves as the ultimate reserve behind the country's currency and banking system, and the U.S. is committed to buy gold at $35 per ounce and to sell it at roughly that figure to foreign central banks and treasuries. This commitment, no less than America's role in international trade and finance, has powerfully shaped the character of present international payments arrangements. Under the Bretton Woods Agreement of 1944, participating nations agreed to value their currencies in either gold *or* dollars, thus setting a broad pattern of stable exchange rates, which, however, can be changed if occasion requires. In addition, the architects of Bretton Woods overtly recognized a practice which had in fact grown up in the 'twenties—namely, that nations might well hold their ultimate exchange reserves, not only in gold but in other foreign currencies, notably the dollar.

Finally, they set up the International Monetary Fund, into which countries put both gold and their own currencies in return for drawing rights on the currencies of other countries when they found themselves in temporary exchange difficulties.

These various escape hatches make the present international monetary system a far less rigorous taskmaster than was the pristine gold standard, when countries were expected to settle their foreign balances promptly in gold, and to adjust their domestic policies promptly to loss or gain of the yellow metal. Nevertheless, under the gold-exchange system nations today cannot go on indefinitely paying out more abroad than they take in. Sooner or later, if imports and other payments exceed exports, they will be under pressure to take remedial action at home by tightening up on credit and making their own currencies more desirable to the rest of the world. The rules of the gold standard have been watered down, and gold these days has to listen to considerable parliamentary palaver before its suggestions are heeded. Yet as Britain discovered in the case of the House of Stuart, even deposed monarchs can exercise a lot of influence behind the scenes, and so it has turned out in monetary matters.

2.

In the immediate post-war years, it was of course other nations and not the U.S. which had to worry about their balance of payments, since U.S. exports and the dollar were riding high, and the U.S. had the only large market where foreign countries could buy needed food, tools, and machinery. But as Europe, in particular, rebuilt its shattered industries, competition inevitably increased, and in the 'fifties a gap began to open in the foreign accounts of the United States. In 1958, this gap widened to some $3.5 billion, and in the period of 1958–63 the total deficit ran to $18.3 billion. At first the deficit was a kind of boon to other nations, allowing them to build up dollar reserves and hence their own internal liquidity. Presently, they began to grow restive at just holding dollars, and in effect financing the United States, and they began to ask for redemption. From 1958 to the end of 1963, the U.S. lost about $7.3 billion in gold, and its total gold stock has declined from a post-war high of over $24 billion in 1949 to less than $16 billion today.

This is still a lot of gold, but the demands against it are also large, since under present law the U.S. needs roughly $13 billion in gold to support its domestic monetary structure. In addition, foreign official and private holdings of short-term dollar claims run to about $22 billion. Thus technically the U.S. is far overdrawn in its gold account. Under the circumstances, it is not surprising that there has been great concern about the U.S. balance of payments gap, which has taken a peculiar shape. In the 'sixties the U.S. has consistently exported more goods than it has imported, and in addition it has derived considerable net revenue from "invisible" service items, if one

counts the interest and dividends paid on U.S. investments previously made abroad. Indeed in 1962, to
take a single year as a point of departure, the U.S. export surplus plus these earnings gave us a favorable
position of some $7 billion. But this surplus was eaten
away and finally turned into a deficit by a large number of offsetting items, including some $2.5 billion
paid out for maintaining U.S. troops and installations
overseas, some $3.5 billion for foreign aid and other
purposes, and finally a large outflow of private long-
term and short-term capital.

Depending on one's preference, one can indict any
one of these items as the "villain" of the piece, and
in fact the government has sought to mitigate each
of them. It has tried, for instance, to persuade foreign nations to buy more military equipment in this
country, and thus offset in part the military outlays
which the U.S. makes and will have to make as long
as it maintains troops in Europe and defends its stra-
tegic interests in southeast Asia. Expenditures for
foreign aid have been in large part "tied" to the purchase of U.S. goods, so that in a roundabout way
they bring back a return in exports. Finally, in 1963
the Kennedy administration launched a direct attack
on private capital outflows by proposing a so-called
"equalization" tax on American purchases of foreign
securities.

Yet of all the measures proposed to date for rem-
edying the balance of payments deficit, this tax
would seem to be the most dangerous. In the first

place, it smacks of imposing exchange controls on the dollar, the ultimate resort of bankrupt official-dom and the favorite resort, incidentally, of dicta-tors. Moreover, the tax overlooks the basic reason why foreign companies have tended to float securi-ties in the American market—namely, that money has been plentiful in the U.S. and interest rates have tended to be lower here than in many other indus-trialized countries. This in turn stems in part from the fact that in the late 'fifties and early 'sixties, de-spite some zigs and zags, the U.S. pursued a rela-tively easy monetary policy, aimed at combating un-employment and slow economic growth at home. Indeed, in the face of persistent deficits and loss of gold, the Federal Reserve sought to "neutralize" its loss by providing fresh reserves to the commercial banking system. In the view of John Exter, senior vice-president of the First National City Bank of New York, this policy was self-defeating, for the world of international money may be compared to a series of interconnecting reservoirs. Increase the availability of money in the U.S. and all that hap-pens is that capital and gold continue to flow abroad, with other countries, not ours, getting the benefit of the monetary stimulus.

One need not take this analysis too literally to believe that tighter money and somewhat higher in-terest rates in the U.S. will tend to mitigate our bal-ance of payments difficulties. In addition, there is little question that persistent budgetary deficits have undermined faith in the dollar, and that the federal budget needs to be swung into balance. Finally, the U.S. should work steadily towards the reduction of costs; and once more the performance of wages is critical, for if wages chew up all productivity gains, both exports and employment will suffer. This approach will be resisted by those who believe that easy money and deficit finance are essential for maintaining U.S. domestic prosperity. Yet even Lord Keynes toward the end of his life had to remind his more ardent followers of the virtues of what he called the "classical medicine," and in broader perspective the U.S. really cannot have it both ways. It cannot maintain its position of leadership and responsibility in the world while at the same time playing fast and loose with the rules. In this matter, we have done a lot of preaching to other nations. It is time to recognize that if we wish the present payments system to work, what is sauce for the goose is sauce for the American gander.

3.

But is the present system of payments itself satisfactory, or is it in need of large-scale overhaul? This is the question that looms just over the horizon of the U.S. balance of payments problem and that, curiously, has been sharpened by the prospect that the U.S. is now putting its external accounts in order. For while the recent outflow of dollars and gold has

been an acute embarrassment to the U.S., it has
greatly strengthened the position of other nations.
What happens when this golden outflow dries up?
According to some highly vocal economists, we
shall then face a "liquidity crisis" in which the world
will run short of basic reserves for financing an increasing volume of international trade and investment.

Such fears seem to me misplaced, and put one in
mind of Mark Twain's remark that the reports of his
death had been "greatly exaggerated." As Mr. Pierre-
Paul Schweitzer, head of the International Monetary
Fund, has remarked with some asperity, "I do not
find any exports or imports which cannot be financed"; and there would seem to be plenty of commercial credit around to do that job. Foreign nations, as we have seen, now possess huge dollar hold-
ings which they are free to use if and when they
find themselves in temporary balance of payments
difficulties. Finally, as Robert V. Roosa, under-
secretary of the U.S. Treasury, has pointed out, the
Bretton Woods system of payments is today far more
expansive and flexible than when it was first initiated.[1] Not only have the resources of the fund been
increased, but nations have been making all kinds of
side arrangements (including so-called "swap agree-
ments") under which they in effect lend out reserves
to each other. All this, in Mr. Roosa's view, has given
the present payments system a new "dimension"

1 *Foreign Affairs* (October, 1963).

which will preclude the kind of "dollar shortage" that occurred in the immediate post-war years.

The truth is that liquidity is not our main problem, and all too often it is used as a kind of fig leaf for covering up a policy of drift and disorder. The real problem is *discipline* and how we choose to enforce it, and this carries the argument into deeper ground. It has long been the contention of Professor Milton Friedman of the University of Chicago that the present system is in fact giving us the worst of all possible worlds.[2] On the one hand, precisely because it is so liquid, it lacks the automaticity of the old gold standard, under which payments deficits had to be promptly settled. On the other hand, fear of losing gold exerts just enough pressure to thwart consistent and rational monetary policies at home which would insure steady growth and employment. In the system as it has developed, the Federal Reserve has so many responsibilities that it fulfills none of them adequately. Instead, the "tail" of international trade and investment tends to wag the "dog" of sound domestic finance.

Professor Friedman would cut through this dilemma by demonitizing gold entirely, adopting at home a fixed rule for increasing the U.S. money supply—say, by 3 to 4 per cent per year—and going over to a system of "floating" exchange rates which would in effect keep our foreign accounts in balance. If,

[2] *A Program for Monetary Reform* (New York: Fordham University Press, 1959).

while the American price level was held stable, the price levels of other nations rose as the result of inflation, the rate on the dollar would go to a premium, thus encouraging U.S. imports and discouraging exports. In contrary circumstances, the dollar would fall in value and imports would decrease and exports increase. The fluctuations in exchange rates would take care of the external payments problem, leaving the U.S. and other nations free to perfect at home dependable and stable monetary arrangements on which businessmen could count.

We may honor Professor Friedman for his pioneering work in monetary theory and for his desire to establish what some have called a true monetary constitution at home, under which we would achieve a less erratic money supply. I am far from persuaded, however, that it is wise or necessary to combine this goal with floating exchange rates. Importers, exporters, and investors count on exchange stability in making their commitments. Fluctuating rates might well intensify currency and trade wars, which we are seeking to avoid. Moreover, unless we are to contemplate very wide swings in exchange rates due to divergent price levels, major countries would have in fact to pursue complementary and coordinated domestic credit policies. But if this would be necessary under a system of floating rates, should we not try for such coordination while maintaining the advantages of fixed rates, rather than introducing a further element of uncertainty into international relations?

It is all very well, perhaps, for smaller countries to adopt floating rates, but are these really appropriate to the major players in the international game?

Such questions lead to a consideration of still another school of thought, which, far from wanting us to relax the discipline of gold, aims at reconstructing a truly modern gold standard. The first objective of this school—represented, among others, by the French economist Jacques Rueff—is to stop the accretion of more dollar claims abroad, and, for that matter, claims on sterling and other currencies, and to settle all future net transactions between nations in gold. The second objective is to wipe out or at least reduce the outstanding dollar claims, which are the cause, it is held, not of stability, but of great instability in the modern world. If this were to be done, however, and if gold were once more to be coined domestically, or at any rate made fully available to private citizens in bullion form, it must be concluded that at present there is not enough gold in the world at its current $35 price to go around, and that not enough is being mined at that price to bring in adequate new reserves of the yellow metal.[3] Gold would have to be repriced to correspond to the rise in world price levels since 1934, and this might in turn mean a fixed gold price in dollars of perhaps $70 per ounce.

This is, to say the least, a very large order, and

[3] Michael A. Heilperin, "The Case for Going Back to Gold," *Fortune* (September, 1962).

the mere proposal of changing the price of gold instantly brings charges of again attempting to "devalue" the dollar and to tear up existing commitments. Some of these charges seem overdrawn. Modern advocates of the gold standard are not advocating that gold be revalued unilaterally, but rather in conjunction with other nations and the International Monetary Fund. Proceeds from the revaluation would largely be used to pay off existing claims on gold, so that, technically at least, the move need not be inflationary. Thirdly, it must be observed that those who today talk most about the sanctity of the present $35 price find themselves in an ambiguous position. We honor gold as the key to the whole existing monetary structure. But so little do we trust present arrangements that we slap people in jail if they even so much as deal in gold without proper license from the authorities! This is, as the saying goes, a very peculiar way to run a railroad.

It is, and the day may well come when gold, instead of being surreptitiously tucked away under the mattress or hoarded in central banks, will once more glitter in the hands of individual citizens. Yet the difficulties of returning to gold coinage at a value consonant with present price levels are immense, and currently at least, I think, almost insurmountable. At the practical level of politics, any change in the gold price must involve extended debate in Congress, during which period—and it might be a long one—the whole world would be in suspense, and it might even be found necessary to suspend gold payments temporarily to avoid the wildest kind of speculation against the dollar (to say nothing of the fact that during the debate we should undoubtedly hear something from the now quiescent silver bloc). Rightly or wrongly, people associate the gold tinkering of the 'thirties, as practiced by President Roosevelt, with irresponsible finance, and psychology may be just as important in this matter as banking techniques. More fundamentally, supposing the transition to the new dispensation could be effected, we should still not be free of the problems which today confront us on the domestic and international scenes. Fiscal and monetary authorities would still be faced with the fact that if wages and costs are pushed up too rapidly, unemployment results unless the economy is reflated upward. Changing the price of gold and the amount of gold in the world neither solves this problem permanently nor makes it go away. If a new gold standard were to work, we should still have to break radically with the orthodoxy which holds that easy money and government spending are the great panaceas for unemployment.

This argues powerfully, it seems to me, not for regarding the present payments system as perfect or for discouraging full and open debate as to how it might be improved, but rather for putting first things first and then taking another fix on where we are. This means curing the chronic and persistent payments deficit of the U.S. by maintaining a dollar

that is not just as good as gold but as *good as goods*—
preventing the constant slow erosion of its purchasing power. Caught up in the intricacies of money, it
is easy to mistake the trees for the wood, and to forget that the best monetary system devisable requires
certain deep-laid foundations if it is to endure at all.
In the case of gold, in particular, it is all too easy to
delude ourselves that the standard *created* the economic freedoms of the nineteenth century and so accounted for the upsurge of economic development
between Waterloo and August, 1914. This is not so.
Rather, the gold standard depended on widespread
acceptance of sound domestic finance, flexibility in
prices and costs, and finally, institutions favoring
freedom of trade and of capital to cross national
boundaries.

4.

This is the kind of world the U.S. should stand for,
especially when we remember how much we owe our
own internal free market—and here one can speak
with a good deal more certainty. The world needs a
continuous expansion of true multi-lateral trade
—trade primarily carried on by *individuals and private corporations,* as contrasted with government-
planned deals such as characterize the Communist
world and all planned systems of economy. Since the
'thirties, the U.S. has made some progress in the matter of reducing tariff barriers, and one purpose of the
Trade Expansion Act of 1962 was to carry this prog-

ress further. Yet a good deal of the political argument for that act was tainted with spurious reasoning. It was argued that the President should have larger powers to negotiate tariff reductions at home lest the U.S. be cut out of foreign markets abroad, notably in the Common Market in Europe. In the context of the U.S. balance of payments deficit this was perhaps only natural, but the argument nevertheless puts the cart before the horse. The enduring argument for free, or at least freer, trade is not just that exporters will gain, but that imports as well as exports will rise, thus benefiting the ultimate consumer, who is every man. Indeed, exports are fundamentally important only as they serve to pay for imports which can be produced relatively more cheaply abroad than they can at home. From this point of view it would pay the U.S. to initiate, if need be unilaterally, a long-term program for reducing and dismantling the whole U.S. quota-tariff wall, which has become an increasing anachronism in the twentieth century.

Such a program would, of course, invite anguished cries from protectionists both in industry and in labor that the U.S. would be "flooded" with the products of "cheap" foreign labor, but it is well to take the measure of such objections. What counts in world trade is not just the level of wages as between country and country but the level of costs, which depend on wage rates *and* productivity; and it so happens that the *general* level of productivity in the

U.S. is still double or more that of European countries and many times that of Japan, which is the basic
reason why our wage rates are higher. From earliest
times it has paid nations of very different living
standards to trade with each other, and were this not
so all trade would have dried up long ago. The
underlying reason for this is that profitable two-way
trade depends not on absolute but on *comparative*
advantage. A businessman may be a good executive
and a good cook, but it still pays him to keep to
business and to hire a cook—to specialize. Just so
with the trade of nations. In the long run, everybody
gains if a country exports the things in which it is
highly efficient and imports the things in which it is
less efficient.

These considerations deflate the argument that
lowering tariffs here would "flood" the country with
foreign goods, to the detriment of U.S. employment.
What is, of course, necessary if the law of comparative advantage is to work fruitfully is the elimination
by monetary means of chronic payments deficits, and
the maintenance of a high degree of flexibility in the
productive structure of national economies. The
progressive elimination of U.S. tariffs would eventually lead to an increase in imports (on some estimates, to $1 to $3 billion per year), and if everything else stayed the same we might of course have
further difficulties in paying our foreign bills. But
everything should not stay the same. In so far as the
new imports were comparatively cheaper than goods

made here, they would tend to benefit the hard-pressed breadwinner. Men put out of work in some industries would move to others, including the export trades. In a dynamic and flexible economy, these are the kind of adjustments that go on at all times. It is only if we conceive of conditions as absolutely static and rigid that the case against freer trade and, for that matter, against freer international investment becomes plausible.

For both the U.S. and the world will benefit as profitable private foreign investment expands, accompanied by a diminution of U.S. foreign economic aid, which is already on the way. In the early 'sixties, as previously noted, the total outflow of U.S. capital was fairly large, but much of this was the movement of short-term funds responding to lack of confidence in the dollar. The creative long-term investment which the U.S. makes abroad takes the form of direct investment by private companies owning facilities overseas (running to about $2.5 billion per year, counting reinvested earnings), as well as some portfolio investment in foreign-owned enterprises. Such creative investment has tended to flow primarily into western Europe and Canada. In less developed areas it tends to be concentrated in the extractive industries, including oil and metals, rather than in other industries which these nations also want and need. Hence the constant assertion in many quarters that while private investment may be all very well, it has little part to play in the economic development and growth of the poorer countries.

Yet the fact is that the investment opportunities in many of these countries have been shut off by their own domestic policies. U.S. private investment in Latin America, for instance, has tended of recent years to decline as the result of the seizure of the tin mines in Bolivia, the putting up of "help not wanted" signs by Argentina and Brazil, and the Sovietizing of Cuba on our doorstep, with all its ramifications throughout the hemisphere. In the Far East, Sukarno's expulsion of the Dutch from Indonesia and later from New Guinea with tacit U.S. approval has not helped the investment climate, and in the Middle East Nasser, having seized the Suez Canal outright, again with the U.S. standing by, has proved more hospitable to aid, whether from Russia or the U.S., than to profit-seeking business. Investment will not flow uphill, and here government policy and diplomacy have a good deal to answer for. Back in 1957 Herman Abs, the German banker, proposed a new Magna Charta calling on all signatory nations to recognize that "everyone has the right to own property alone or in association with others" and proposing a new kind of world court to adjudicate property disputes. That proposal or some form of it should be taken off the shelf and implemented. Were this done, there might well be a much larger flow of private capital into the backward nations and those now seeking their new place in the sun.

Concomitantly, we should rethink and redirect and, in the end, reduce the multiple programs of foreign aid that have grown like Topsy over the years in Washington. It may be provident to give arms and dollar assistance to countries that, whatever their internal policies, stand on the firing line against Communist aggression. But it is self-defeating to scatter foreign aid to Indonesia or Algeria, which look to Moscow for their basic orientation. Such largesse comes pretty close to knuckling under to blackmail. In the matter of straight economic assistance to backward nations, we would be wise, I think, to channel what we have to give through the World Bank for International Development, which has proved its worth. Much less can be said for loans and grants which are now being made directly by the U.S. government. To the degree that these are continued at all, they should be made conditional on the receiving country adopting monetary and economic policies which give some hope for success.

It is often argued that the poorer nations of the world need an "infra-structure" of roads, railroads, harbor development, and the like, which free enterprise cannot supply. But it is also true that if the governments of these nations ceased pouring money into basic industries like steel, they would have more tax receipts for financing roads and other public facilities. In this matter, India is a case in point. Under its five-year plan, the government has pressed for the development of heavy industry at whatever cost, and then it has turned to the U.S. and the outside world for assistance to balance its external accounts. But the government program has in itself been inflationary, and the main cause of balance of payments difficulties. As economist B. R. Shenoy of India has argued, India might well raise private money abroad were its own currency strong. And as he and others have pointed out, large government-to-government transactions simply help rivet onto developing countries a form of socialism.[4]

In sum, the great task of the U.S. is to project outward the principles which have on the evidence contributed so much to our own development from colonial times into the twentieth century—respect for private property, belief in the efficacy of the market, and the maintenance of strong but limited government. In doing so, we should see to it that the further unification of the world depends, not on elaborate inter-government deals, but rather on the maintenance of channels through which individuals and peoples come to deal with each other. An American businessman doing business in the Ruhr may be indirectly contributing more to U.S.-West German relations than the occasional meeting of the President and the Chancellor. The house of W. R. Grace has probably contributed far more to U.S.-Latin American relations over the years than all the sound and fury poured into the Alliance for Progress. This is not to underrate the role of governments in main-

[4] "The Right Road to Indian Progress," *Fortune* (April, 1960).

taining the framework within which individuals can operate. As we have seen, there is indeed an unfinished task here, especially in the matter of developing an international monetary system. But even this unfinished task must be seen in the perspective of a broader panorama. One of the greatest economists of our time, the late D. H. Robertson, has compared the role of money to that of a highway which joins together the productive resources of the earth and puts them at the disposal of the ultimate consumer, who is every man, rich and poor. But having paid his respects to the importance of money, Robertson then significantly concludes: "The mending of the road over which produce passes to market is no substitute for the digging and dunging of the fields themselves."[5]

[5] *Money* (New York: Harcourt, Brace & World, Inc., 1929).

CHAPTER IX

Of the American mission

"We have no empire of the mind as yet."
—R. W. DAVENPORT, *My Country*

THE CHALLENGE THAT CONFRONTS the
United States in seeking to build an international order favorable to private trade and investment brings
us home to the underlying thesis of this book. Governments have a vast and complicated role to play in
maintaining the institutional framework in which
economic activity and much else can flourish and expand, but they cannot seek to direct the whole process without fatally compromising the very ends and
purposes of human and humane endeavor. "I have
been over to the future and it works," said Lincoln
Steffens in 1919, after his first visit to the Soviet
Union. Returning from Moscow recently, forty years
after the great Revolution, another American journalist, Henry Grunwald, confessed himself tempted
to reverse that dictum: "I have been over to the past
and it has failed."

Why failed? Not because the Soviets have not labored with might and main to increase production, for in this they have to some degree succeeded. Not because they have chosen until recently, at least, to devote a high proportion of their energies to increasing the output of capital goods at the expense of consumer goods, with the idea that some day the investment will pay off in a gigantic outpouring of cars, refrigerators, clothing, and appurtenances for the proletariat. The failure goes much deeper. In one way or another, the Soviet system has cut the nexus which in the free economy binds the production of goods to the will and desires of the consumer, so that even where consumer goods are produced today in Russia they are shoddy and ill-fitted to human needs. The chief characteristic of Soviet life, according to many accounts, is its total drabness. Its further characteristic is that nobody seems to care about serving anybody else, or has much incentive for so doing since it is the reputed function of the state to say what shall be produced and what shall be consumed. Is this really so surprising? For the premise of dialectical materialism, after all, is an historic determinism in which individual desires and aspirations do not really count.

In any case, we have the paradox that the new Soviet utopia, which places all emphasis on material things, runs short of wheat, whereas in the West, and particularly in the U.S., a new age of abundance is already manifest. Writing in the mid-nineteenth century, Marx and Engels thought they were burying capitalism. Before lowering the coffin they pronounced a prophetic eulogy at its graveside. "The bourgeoisie," they wrote in the Communist Manifesto, "during its rule of scarce one hundred years has created more massive and more colossal productive forces than have all preceding generations together. Subjection of nature's forces to man, machinery, application of chemistry to industry and agriculture, steam navigation, railways, electric telegraphs, clearing of whole continents for cultivation, canalization of rivers, whole populations conjured out of the ground—what earlier century had even a presentiment that such productive forces slumbered in the lap of social labor?"[1]

What indeed! Yet the trouble with this tribute to the era, which in America ended with the Mexican War and the California gold rush, is that it applies equally well to the century which followed these events—the century which saw the invention of the internal combustion engine, the automobile, and the airplane; the application of electric power and the discovery of oil; the rise of radio, radar, television, modern chemistry, and now atomic fission. It was given to Marx, the close student of capitalism, to understand almost everything about it except its essential promise. That promise is not to exploit but in a profound sense to liberate—to liberate men from poverty and from grinding toil, and to liberate them, for the "pursuit of happiness," and, let us hope, for the pursuit of virtue.

This is likewise the declared purpose of our po-

1 *Handbook of Marxism* (New York: Random House, Inc., 1935).

litical institutions, without which the free economy could never have evolved. For capitalism, or, more precisely, the market-property economy, as we have been at pains to emphasize, is not self-sustaining but requires an "envelope of law" which it is the function of government to supply. When we say that we hold for a government of law and not men, we mean precisely a government that lays down the rules under which economic activity and much else goes forward. We need not re-emphasize here the magnitude of the task that falls on the government of a republic in its role of rule-maker, not only in the international but in the national sphere. We may be permitted to stress again that what counts is not primarily the size of government, though that is important, but its quality, and that, given the nature of the coercive power of all government, we should intelligently seek to ration its functions. The blessing of federalism is that it takes off the back of centralized government tasks that can better be performed by the states and local communities. The blessing inherent in our economic system is that it allows people to do for themselves what governments, however wise and benevolent, cannot possibly do for them.

2.

The question remains whether a Commonwealth, so conceived, and an economy, so conceived, can continue to rise to the challenges of modernity, whose law is flux and rapid change. At the material and economic level, I believe that the long-term prognosis is hopeful as long as we keep a grip on what makes material progress possible, and maintain a due sense of perspective. The outer world is still a desperately poor place, and the need of underdeveloped nations for both capital and trade is well-nigh limitless. Slowly and gradually, we may hope, they too will evolve the economic and political institutions which can make the assuagement of those needs possible. In the U.S. itself there is still too much poverty, though the statistics, for what they are worth, are by no means discouraging. It seems likely that only a generation ago nearly half of the American people were "poor" by today's standards. In a revealing study made some years ago, Professor Robert J. Lampman of the University of Wisconsin estimated that in 1947 some 26 per cent of the U.S. population was below the poverty line. By 1957, the figure had fallen to 19 per cent, or, in his telling phrase, "one-fourth of the way towards zero." More recent estimates, based on a higher income standard, indicate that the reduction of poverty since then has been less rapid, and that the poor still constitute roughly one-fifth of an otherwise affluent society.

This is surely too much by any standard, nor should we allow the statistical advance to blind us to the inhumane conditions that exist in our city slums, in part of our agricultural economy, and in the ramshackle buildings that rise not too far from the Capitol dome in Washington. Yet a single, grandiose "war on poverty" on the part of the federal government would seem to be ill-suited to the nature of the problem—the more so when one considers that the poor include the old, the young, the displaced industrial worker, and the underemployed cotton picker of the deep South. On the contrary, if government is to contribute anything to solving the problem its means must be selective, and it should furthermore be realized that what is spent at the federal level—be it $500 million or $2 billion—is literally a drop in the bucket. The redistribution of income through taxation and other means is no substitute for the increase in real incomes all around. What has reduced poverty in the past from half of the nation to the present fifth is the increased output of goods and services guided by a system which maintains incentives, fosters industrial competition, and leads through a natural rather than a forced-draft process to the investment of savings in productive capital equipment. In our anxiety to help those below the poverty line, we must be careful not to impair the system which already puts 150 million Americans above that line, and can raise many more above the line tomorrow.

Paradoxically, it is the fact that poverty can only be conquered in the long run by increasing man-hour productivity on farm and in factory through the use of better tools and larger investment, which gives rise to many present-day fears: the fear of *over*-production, of technological unemployment, and of the machine itself. On the first point, as has been made plain, we are very far from having conquered the business cycle at home, and in the national no less than in the international sphere there are deep monetary problems still to be resolved. Yet on the longer view, I think we have paid a heavy price for cultivating the notion that economic demand must always be deficient, given rising supply.

For in a profound sense production is demand. It is the money which I earn at a job which gives me the buying power to purchase goods made by others, and I hold a job precisely because I produce something of value. Indeed if we strip aside the intricacies of money we find that all goods and services are paid for by other goods and services. What makes exchange profitable is that A has something which B wants and B makes something which A wants. As formulated by the famous economist, Jean Baptiste Say, in the nineteenth century, this so-called law of markets was no doubt crudely expressed and needs refinement. If the law is to hold, it is necessary that all factors of production and all goods and services be correctly *priced.* It is also necessary that what people save pass over smoothly into investment outlay, which, in the view of the late Lord Keynes, was by no means certain or assured. Yet when all the qualifications are in it is safer, I think, to suppose that production in a market economy is correlated with demand than it is to suppose that they are entirely separate entities, as has been the modern fashion. For were this so, all economic progress would have stalled long ago. As the economist W. H. Hutt has observed: "Demands in general can be deficient only as supply is withheld."[2] We must see that supply is not withheld by the monopoly pricing of goods or labor, or by other roadblocks. But this is an argument for perfecting the competitive market within a sound monetary framework, rather than for destroying it by constant inflation and monetary debasement.

The same conclusion emerges in the matter of technological unemployment, which today commands the headlines. No one who has visited the Appalachian coal-mining towns will doubt their distress, and the need for state and local measures to assuage it—and the larger need for preventing its recurrence. Yet as argued in Chapter V, much depends on how technological innovation is handled. If machines are introduced simply as an embattled response to wage increases already made, the results may be cruel. But if the fruits of technology are passed on in the form of lower consumer prices and better products, new machines in effect create new jobs. The world has rolled over many times since the Luddites early in the nineteenth century sought to smash up the new textile machinery then being installed. From their immediate point of view, the workers had reason to fear this development. In larger context, we can see that those fears were misplaced.

[2] W. H. Hutt, *Keynesianism—Retrospect and Prospect* (Chicago: Henry Regnery Company, 1963).

If the introduction of machinery really led to the diminution of employment, we should all of us have been out of work long ago, including those of us who use the humble typewriter. Watching the modern bulldozer at work, we wonder sometimes what has become of all the men who once worked with pick and shovel—until we remind ourselves that were it not for the bulldozer the ground in question would probably never have been cleared, and the new housing development never started. Reading of the wonders of the computer, one can likewise conjure up a world where even the manager, to say nothing of the worker, has been disposed of—until again one reflects that without the computer there would be no emerging space industry and no moon shot.

"Civilization," wrote Alfred North Whitehead, "advances by extending the number of important operations which we can perform without thinking about them."[3] If this is true then the computer must be hailed, not only for simplifying the management of business inventories, but also for relieving the scientist and the engineer of an intolerable amount of pedestrian calculation which has little to do with creative thinking. And let those who fear the computer take heart for another reason, since like most great inventions it is not so revolutionary after all. Its modern development is generally attributed to the work of Howard Aiken and to International

[3] Alfred North Whitehead, *Introduction to Mathematics* (London, 1911).

Business Machines. But Aiken, it turns out, simply finished the work begun over a century ago by that crusty Englishman Charles Babbage, who put together a machine called the "analytical engine." And Babbage, it turns out, was not only an admirer of the lovely Lady Lovelace, daughter of Lord Byron, but an even greater admirer of the father of the free market, Adam Smith!

3.

The real threat of the computer, I suspect, is not what it will do to employment but what it could do to our thinking about the needs of society in an increasingly complex world. Leafing through some scientific periodicals, one is vaguely and uncomfortably reminded of the claims of the Technocrats who burst into temporary prominence in the early 'thirties. It was the argument of the Technocrats that the advances of the physical sciences had obsoleted the need for a market economy based on prices and monetary values. It was up to the scientists, or a few of them, to draw up blueprints for what should be produced and in what quantities, based on estimates and extrapolations of the so-called rational needs of the population. It is sad to recall that such "scientific" planning was favored, not only by many writers of the day, but by such a famous historian as the late Charles A. Beard; and it is appalling to find these ideas re-echoed today by Harold Wilson, head of

Britain's Labor party, who has said that all that Britain needs is a little more science and technology. On the evidence, Britain needs much more than that if her political economy is to remain solvent and if her people are to remain free.

The great fallacy of the Technocrats, and of all who believe that we can be saved by a little more "social engineering," is a false appreciation of the true nature of man's economic problem. That problem, as we have emphasized, is not just to produce more goods and services, but to produce the goods and services that people want and freely choose—*to enlarge the scope of human options*. The engineer, to take a simple example, can tell us how to design an automobile. It is not up to the engineer to tell us that what we really want and need is a better house. Yet when man acts economically he must make such choices, and how he decides is determined in the last analysis by his taste and preference. Engineering deals essentially with means; economics deals with the problem of how scarce means shall be deployed to alternative ends; it is shot through and through with human and, we may hope, humane evaluations. As Lord Robbins reminded us many years ago in his essay on *The Nature and Significance of Economic Science*,[4] the task of economics begins just where technology leaves off, and to confuse these tasks could be, in his view, "one of the main dangers of civilization."

4 (London: Macmillan & Co., Ltd., 1935).

It is the function of the free economy to allow human judgments and values to be registered in the market place, and in an age of rapid technological innovation we shall need its services more, not less. If war is too important to be left to the generals, choice as to what shall be produced, saved, invested, and consumed is too important to be left to the scientists, or to any group of reputed "experts." Indeed, there is great danger in the idea that because our problems are complex, the experts can decide them and all will be well. But all will not be well. As we have seen, experts can work out ingenious formulas for how fast the country should grow. It does not follow that the means they would apply are viable in a free society. Experts can no doubt solve the country's balance of payments problem by instituting exchange controls, but such controls will swiftly stultify free trade and investment. Experts may conjure away the country's abounding farm surpluses by recommending ever more stringent production restraints, but such restraints have their own hidden and intangible costs. Economic life can be organized as in the Soviet Union through specific government dictate. Or it can be organized through a system giving scope to free collaboration and individual choice. At issue when all the arguments are in and when the experts have had their say is a moral question— namely, the *value* we place on liberty itself, and on the ultimate nature and purpose of human life.

4.

It is on the answer given to this ultimate question, seemingly far removed from the busy hum of factory floor and of noisy political debate, that the future of the U.S. and of the civilization of which we are a part will turn. From the seventeenth century forward, we have been riding the wave of ever more dazzling discoveries made through the methodology of the natural sciences. Today those sciences are not as sure as they were in the days of Newton as to the nature of the physical universe. Yet at this very time the so-called "social sciences" are presenting us with an all-too-sure view of man's makeup and nature. In the view of crude behaviorist psychology, man is no more than a complex of behavioral "patterns" which are determined by his external environment. Consciousness, choice, values, emotions, desires—all fade out of the picture, and are explained away by physical stimuli and physical responses. On this view of human nature, it is not too difficult to compare man to the modern computer, and to foresee a day when the computer will have, so to speak, made man obsolete.

Yet this view of man and his destiny actually embodies a fallacy as old as Democritus—that because man has a body and a brain and lives in a physical universe, that is all there is to him. We expect this kind of nonsense from devout Marxian materialists, but it comes as a shock when it is seriously put forward in modern dress by so-called social scientists. In that extraordinary little book, *The Measure of Man*,[5] Joseph Wood Krutch remarks on the paradox that while "many physicists have given free will back to the atoms . . . sociologists still seem to deny it to the human being"; and he goes on tartly to suggest that "the Sciences of Man might do well to accept a little more freely than they seem inclined to do the possibility that man himself is at least as mysterious as a lump of uranium." That is to put the point mildly. More positively, we can be sure that any definition of man which leaves out choice and the significance of moral and religious values is a kind of intellectual humbug.

What is needed at the highest intellectual level, no doubt, it is not just more physics but a modern *metaphysics* which would find a place for teleological purpose in our affairs, and which could reconcile and relate the fragmented disciplines which multiply day by day in our universities. Meantime, while awaiting the deliverance of the philosophers, we shall have to stumble along as best we can with the old "eternal" verities. Are they so bad, however hackneyed—belief in the "divine spark," belief in the "dignity of man," belief that men are "endowed by their Creator with certain inalienable rights"? They will have to do, at least for the time being, if we are to retain our grip on what does truly separate the clanking materialism

5 (New York: Grosset & Dunlap Universal Library, 1954).

of communism from our own way of life, if we are to perfect our political and economic institutions, if we are to realize the promise of what has variously been called the "American Century," the "American purpose," the "American mission."

What is that mission after all? To maintain a sheltering shield of military power against the further encroachment of tyranny, and to roll back and neutralize those who have said they will bury us; to build behind that shield through the principle of federalism a more united Atlantic community; to project outward the rule of law and liberty under the law which has been both our inheritance and our pride; to shape not only a more prosperous America but an America that, in the phrase of John F. Kennedy, "will not be afraid of grace and beauty"; to use the promise of the machine, not just for the conquest of poverty, but for the pursuit of excellence and distinction. Great tasks require great builders, and the mission of America is to build no less than to defend. Yet, in the clamorous and busy world of tomorrow, let us hope too that there will be time for reflection in those silent and indeed lonely hours when the spirit reasserts its influence and reanimates the human endeavor. America is not a purpose but purposes, not an ideal but ideals, not a crowd but men and women. It will be in the heart and mind of each one that the future of the Republic will be shaped, its premises vindicated, and its promises fulfilled.

Appendix I

Note on unemployment statistics

While the gravest kind of decisions are these days made in Washington on the basis of unemployment statistics, these statistics are more inflated and tricky than the casual reader of the newspapers would assume. Specifically, the most commonly used figure—namely, the percentage of unemployed to the labor force—is so unreliable that it should practically be disregarded in determining short-run policy.

The reason resides in the manner in which employment, unemployment, and labor force figures are calcualted. In most European countries, unemployment is measured in terms of men and women registering with a government agency to find work and/or to draw unemployment insurance. The U.S. uses a more generous approach. Each month the Bureau of the Census surveys some 35,000 households in the U.S. and in effect asks their members: Are you at work or are you looking for work? On the basis of this spot check the government then issues three key figures: (1) the number of people over fourteen years old who are employed, (2) the number who are seeking jobs and are unemployed, and (3) the civilian labor force, which is simply the addition of the above two figures.

The key point is that all *three* of these figures are variables by definition, and subject to peculiar variations. In good times the employment figure will go up as heads of families who may have been temporarily out of work find jobs. But housewives and older men may also decide to try to earn some extra money and, depending on their luck, will either swell the employment or the unemployment figure. In bad times the head of the family may be out of work, but again, some of his dependents may be seeking work, thus pushing up the unemployment figure. U.S. accounting methods have something to do with the fact that whereas unemployment in Britain has been running to between 2 and 3 per cent of the labor force, unemployment in the U.S. has been running to 5 or 6 per cent, and some years ago it was estimated that if Sweden used the U.S. method its unemployment would have tripled.

Even taking the U.S. figures at face value, it is important to interpret them correctly. In our big economy it is normal for some 4 to 5 per cent of the labor force to be seeking jobs as the result of moving about the country and switching from one task to another. Hence concern for unemployment has recently narrowed to a margin of 1 per cent or 2 per cent of the total working force. The "hard core" of unemployment, typified by displaced miners, is centered in those who have been out of work over long periods —say, six months or more. In addition, there is great variation in unemployment, as between groups and classes. In the good times of 1963–64, there was little unemployment slack among skilled adults, and indeed, demand for such workers in some communities tended to outrun supply.

Over the years, unemployment has tended to be relatively high among unskilled workers and Negroes, partly because of discriminatory practices, but also partly because minimum wage laws have set uneconomic rates and have done more harm than good. Unemployment has also tended to be high among the younger age groups, causing great concern because this class of the population is growing rapidly. In part, however, it is normal for those seeking work for the first time to experience some difficulty in landing a "break-in" job, and if a more youthful labor force is a challenge, it is also a promise. In the whole matter of growth the least publicized figures are probably the most important—namely, that in the single decade of 1950–60 actual civilian employment grew from 60 to 67 million. If this expansion is to continue, we shall do well to realize that the business of business is not to "create jobs" but to produce goods and services in rising volume and at cheaper prices.

Appendix II

Note on money

Attempts to describe the modern money system are handicapped by the fact that they annoy the sophisticate without necessarily enlightening the unitiated. The latter is referred to any standard economic textbook or to an immensely useful booklet put out by the Federal Reserve Board, *The Reserve System: Purposes and Functions.* For a nominal price the reader will expand his knowledge many times over, and such multiple expansion is, of course, the basic characteristic of our currency and banking system.

In reading Chapters VI and VIII, the reader should be reminded that the national gold stock—omitting gold in commercial use—is held by the U.S. Treasury. The Treasury in its turn issues "gold certificates" to the nation's twelve federal reserve banks. Under present law, federal reserve banks must hold a 25 per cent gold certificate "cover" against their issue of federal reserve notes, which constitute a large part of our currency, and against the reserve deposits which member commercial banks are required to keep with the Federal Reserve. Thus $1 in gold can theoretically sustain $4 in federal reserve notes or commercial bank reserves.

These reserve balances are sometimes called "high-powered money" because they can in their turn sustain a large expansion of commercial bank deposits held by the public and used in checking accounts. This expansion takes place as bankers put part of their funds to work by making loans to individuals or corporations, or by purchasing securities. For when a banker makes you a loan, in effect he opens up a checking account to your order in return for your promissory note. The checking account constitutes *new* deposit money in the system. This kind of expansion is limited by the fact that bankers must maintain a certain ratio between their deposits and their reserves. In the case of large city banks, this reserve requirement currently runs to 16.5 per cent, or one-sixth of demand deposits.

It would thus appear that $1 in gold in the Treasury can in theory sustain, not just $4 in bank reserves, but $24 in member bank deposits. In fact, however, the multiple is considerably less than that since much cash and currency is held by the public and so is not available to the commercial banks as reserves. It should also be noted that, despite the great expansion of the money system, the federal reserve banks still have more gold certificates on hand than legally needed to meet their domestic liabilities,

as distinguished from the nation's huge foreign liabilities. *In extremis,* Congress could of course change the
"gold cover" clause, or, for that matter, eliminate it
entirely. In this case the domestic link to gold would
be gone, though the metal would still be used in
settling international balances. What effects this
would have on confidence in the dollar, on which so
much depends, would, to say the least, be unpredict-
able.

General bibliography

Backman, Jules, *Wage Determination: An Analysis of Wage Criteria*. Princeton: D. Van Nostrand Co., Inc., 1959.

Ballve, Faustino, *Essentials of Economics: A Brief Survey of Principles and Policies,* Arthur Goddard, trans. and ed. Princeton: D. Van Nostrand Co., Inc., 1963.

Berle, Adolf A., Jr., *The American Economic Republic*. New York: Harcourt, Brace & World, Inc., 1963.

Berle, Adolf A., Jr. and Gardiner C. Means, *The Modern Corporation and Private Property*. New York: The Macmillan Company, 1935.

Beveridge, Lord, *Full Employment in a Free Society*. New York: George Allen & Unwin, 1944.

Boarman, Patrick M., *Union Monopolies and Antitrust Restraints*. Washington, D.C.: Labor Policy Association, 1963.

Bradley, Philip D., ed., *The Public Stake in Union Power*. Charlottesville, Va.: University of Virginia Press, 1959.

193

Bryce, James, *The American Commonwealth*. London: Macmillan & Company, Ltd., 1888.

Burgess, W. Randolph, *The Reserve Banks and the Money Market*. New York: Harper & Row, Publishers, 1936.

Chamberlain, John, *The Enterprising Americans: A Business History of the United States*. New York: Harper & Row, Publishers, 1963.

Chamberlin, Edward, *The Theory of Monopolistic Competition: A Reorientation of the Theory of Value*. Cambridge: Harvard University Press, 1936.

Davenport, R. W., *The Dignity of Man*. New York: Harper & Row, Publishers, 1955.

Dewhurst, J. Frederic and associates, *America's Needs and Resources*. New York: The Twentieth Century Fund, 1955.

Dietze, Gottfried, *In Defence of Property*. Chicago: Henry Regnery Company, 1963.

Douglas, Paul H., *The Theory of Wages*. New York: Augustus M. Kelley, 1957.

Eastman, Max, *Reflections on the Failure of Socialism*. New York: The Devin-Adair Co., 1955.

Fairchild, Fred Rogers, Edgar Stevenson Furniss, and Norman Sydney Buck, *Elementary Economics*, 4th ed. New York: The Macmillan Company, 1939.

Fellner, William, *Emergence and Content of Modern Economic Analysis*. New York: McGraw-Hill Book Co., Inc., 1960.

Fortune Editors, *Markets of the Sixties.* New York: Harper & Row, Publishers, 1960.

Friedman, Milton, *Capitalism and Freedom.* Chicago: University of Chicago Press, 1962.

————, *A Program for Monetary Stability.* New York: Fordham University Press, 1959.

Friedman, Milton and Anna Jacobson Schwartz, *A Monetary History of the United States, 1867–1960.* Princeton: Princeton University Press, 1963.

Galbraith, John Kenneth, *The Affluent Society.* Boston: Houghton Mifflin Company, 1958.

————, *The Great Crash, 1929.* New York: Time Inc., Book Division, 1961.

Goldwater, Barry, *The Conscience of a Conservative.* New York: Macfadden-Bartell Corp., 1960.

Gregory, Charles, *Labor and the Law,* 2nd ed. New York: W. W. Norton & Company, Inc., 1958.

Groseclose, Elgin, *Money and Man: A Survey of Monetary Experience.* New York: Frederick Ungar Publishing Co., Inc., 1961.

Haberler, Gottfried von, *Prosperity and Depression: A Theoretical Analysis of Cyclical Movements.* Geneva: League of Nations, 1937.

Hansen, Alvin Harvey, *Business-Cycle Theory: Its Development and Present Status.* Boston: Ginn & Company, 1927.

————, *Fiscal Policy and Business Cycles.* New York: W. W. Norton & Company, Inc., 1941.

Hayek, Friedrich A., *The Constitution of Liberty.* Chicago: University of Chicago Press, 1960.

————, *Individualism and the Economic Order*. Chicago: University of Chicago Press, 1948.

————, *The Road to Serfdom*. Chicago: University of Chicago Press, 1944.

Hazlitt, Henry, ed., *The Critics of Keynesian Economics*. Princeton: D. Van Nostrand Co., Inc., 1960.

————, *The Failure of the "New Economics": An Analysis of the Keynesian Fallacies*. Princeton: D. Van Nostrand Co., Inc., 1959.

Heilbroner, Robert L. and Peter L. Bernstein, *A Primer on Government Spending*. New York: Random House, Inc., 1963.

Hicks, J. R., *The Theory of Wages*. London: Macmillan & Co., Ltd., 1935.

Hutt, W. H., *Keynesianism—Retrospect and Prospect: A Critical Restatement of Basic Economic Principles*. Chicago: Henry Regnery Company, 1963.

————, *The Theory of Collective Bargaining*. Glencoe, Ill.: Free Press of Glencoe, Inc., 1954.

Jacobsson, Per, *The Market Economy in the World of Today*. Philadelphia: American Philosophical Society, 1961.

Jewkes, John, *Ordeal by Planning*. New York: The Macmillan Company, 1948.

Kaplan, A. D. H., *Big Enterprise in a Competitive System*. Washington, D.C.: The Brookings Institution, 1954.

Kendall, Willmoore, *The Conservative Affirmation*. Chicago: Henry Regnery Company, 1963.

Keynes, John Maynard, *The Economic Consequences of the Peace*. New York: Harcourt, Brace & World, Inc., 1920.

———, *Essays in Persuasion*. New York: Harcourt, Brace and World, Inc., 1932.

———, *The General Theory of Employment, Interest and Money*. New York: Harcourt, Brace and World, Inc., 1936.

Krutch, Joseph Wood, *The Measure of Man*. New York: Grosset & Dunlap Universal Library, 1954.

Labor Unions and Public Policy. Washington, D.C.: American Enterprise Association, 1958.

Lindblom, Charles E., *Unions and Capitalism*. New Haven: Yale University Press, 1949.

Lippmann, Walter, *The Good Society*. New York: Grosset & Dunlap Universal Library, 1956.

———, *The Public Philosophy*. Boston: Little, Brown and Company, 1955.

Marshall, Alfred, *Principles of Economics: An Introductory Volume*, 8th ed. London: Macmillan & Co., Ltd., 1936.

Meade, J. E., *An Introduction to Economic Analysis and Policy*. Oxford: The Clarendon Press, 1936.

Meyer, Frank S., *In Defense of Freedom: A Conservative Credo*. Chicago: Henry Regnery Company, 1962.

———, *What Is Conservatism?* New York: Holt, Rinehart and Winston, Inc., 1964.

Mises, Ludwig von, *Human Action: A Treatise on Economics*. New Haven: Yale University Press, 1949.

————, *The Theory of Money and Credit*, 2nd ed., H. E. Batson, trans. New Haven: Yale University Press, 1953.

Morley, Felix, *Freedom and Federalism*. Chicago: Henry Regnery Company, 1959.

Petro, Sylvester, *The Labor Policy of the Free Society*. New York: The Ronald Press Company, 1957.

————, *Power Unlimited: The Corruption of Union Leadership*. New York: The Ronald Press Company, 1959.

Rappard, William E., *The Secret of American Prosperity*. New York: Greenberg, 1955.

Robbins, Lionel, *Economic Planning and International Order*. London: Macmillan & Co., Ltd., 1938.

————, *The Economist in the Twentieth Century and Other Lectures in Political Economy*. London: Macmillan & Co., Ltd., 1954.

————, *An Essay on the Nature and Significance of Economic Science*, 2nd ed. New York: The Macmillan Company, 1935.

————, *The Great Depression*. New York: The Macmillan Company, 1936.

————, *The Theory of Economic Policy: In English Classical Political Economy*. London: Macmillan & Co., Ltd., 1952.

Robertson, D. H., *Money*. New York: Harcourt, Brace and World, Inc., 1929.

Robinson, Claude, *Understanding Profits*. Princeton.: D. Van Nostrand Co., Inc., 1961.

Roepke, Wilhelm, *Economics of the Free Society*, Patrick M. Boarman, trans. Chicago: Henry Regnery Company, 1963.

————, *A Humane Economy: The Social Framework of the Free Market*, Elizabeth Henderson, trans. Chicago: Henry Regnery Company, 1960.

Rueff, Jacques, *The Age of Inflation*. Chicago: Henry Regnery Company, 1964.

Samuelson, Paul A., *Economics: An Introductory Analysis*. 5th ed. New York: McGraw-Hill Book Co., Inc., 1961.

Scherman, Harry, *The Promises Men Live By*. New York: Random House, Inc., 1938.

Simons, Henry C., *Economic Policy for a Free Society*. Chicago: University of Chicago Press, 1948.

Smith, Adam, *An Inquiry into the Wealth of Nations*. London: Oxford University Press, 1880.

Stolper, Gustav, *This Age of Fable*. New York: Reynal & Company, Inc., 1942.

Taylor, Overton H., *A History of Economic Thought*. New York: McGraw-Hill Book Co., Inc., 1960.

Triffin, Robert, *Gold and the Dollar Crisis: The Future of Convertibility*. New Haven: Yale University Press, 1961.

United States Monetary Policy: Its Contribution to Prosperity without Inflation. New York: The American Assembly, Columbia University, 1958.

Wallich, Henry C., *The Cost of Freedom: A New Look at Capitalism*. New York: Harper & Row, Publishers, 1960.

Whitehead, Alfred North, *Science and the Modern World*. New York: The Macmillan Company, 1929.

Wicksteed, Philip H., *The Common Sense of Political Economy*. London: Routledge & Kegan Paul, Ltd., 1935.

Woytinsky, W. S. and associates, *Employment and Wages in the United States*. New York: Twentieth Century Fund, 1953.

Wright, David McCord, *Capitalism*. Chicago: Henry Regnery Company, Gateway Editions, 1962.

———, *A Key to Modern Economics*. New York: The Macmillan Company, 1954.

———, *The Keynesian System*. New York: Fordham University Press, 1961 (The Millar Lectures, No. 4).

Yeager, Leland B., ed., *In Search of a Monetary Constitution*. Cambridge: Harvard University Press, 1962.

Index